D0908033

10-50

CHRIST
OUR
REVELATION

CHRIST
OUR
REVELATION

by

Jeanne Guyon

CHRIST
OUR
REVELATION

by
Jeanne Guyon

Copyright
MCMLXXXV
by
Christian Books
Publishing House

Printed in the
United States of America

Christian Books Publishing House
Box 959
Gardiner, Maine 04345

EDITOR'S PREFACE
PLEASE READ

Do not expect your usual interpretation of the Book of Revelation as you tread herein. Don't even expect to recognize the Book of Revelation as it is viewed in our age. What you are about to read was first written almost exactly 300 years ago (September, 1683). There has never been an interpretation of Revelation — before or since — like this one. It is unique.

Perhaps a little history of the different interpretations of Revelation is in order.

In the latter part of the first century and in the early part of the second century the Book of Revelation had essentially one interpretation: The Roman Empire vs. the Church of Jesus Christ! Revelation was a very current book to these people. The things recorded in it were happening to them — at that moment. There was little in it that was considered futuristic. The message of Revelation was written for them in their present situation and they knew it!

Interest in Revelation waned with the fall of the Roman Empire. That eclipse lasted — essentially — until 1790 ... believe it or not.

Even the Protestant Reformation failed to stir much interest in Revelation. Some few passages, yes, but not the book, nor eschatology (i.e., the study of last things) in general, although Luther was fond of depicting the Pope as the monster who ruled over "the city on seven hills"!

It was the French Revolution that resurrected interest in Revelation. (Guyon had written her book over 100 years earlier!) The French Revolution – and the Reign of Terror – scared the wits out of the whole populace of Great Britain, including its clergy. The preachers of England and Wales saw some horrible thing about to happen to England. (It never came. They were wrong!) They literally saw Revelation as a book written for England, years 1790 through 1800! Before you laugh too loudly, hear this: The next series of interpretations saw Revelation as a book written (exclusively!) for the period between 1800 and 1840. Then came 1840–1880. World War I was a heyday for Revelation. So was World War II! There are those of us still alive who can remember the preachers of Britain and America proclaiming with all certainty that Hitler and Mussolini were the star performers of the Book of Revelation.

And if you are reading this preface in the year 2999, it is a good bet your generation believes wholly in the futuristic interpretation of Revelation and that – surely – it was written solely for your day! This "today's headlines are in Revelation" gets to be a bit silly when stretched over 50 years of one's lifetime, but it does sell books!

Here is our point: Today's generally accepted view of Revelation is only about 200 years old, yet it is so accepted and so engrained in our minds that we accept it as final, incontestable fact!

Today's view of Revelation may be popular . . . true . . . but it is still only an interpretation . . . not inspired dogma, carved in stone on the foundational slabs of the New Jerusalem! The truth is, all interpretations of Revelation are speculations at best, and would be more wisely labeled as sheer guesswork! No one is certain what Revelation means. (As one seminary professor liked to put it: "If the angels don't know when the Lord is returning, it is a sure bet no Baptist preacher knows!")

When Jeanne Guyon wrote this book, it was 100 years before any clear ground rules for approaching Revelation had been laid down. Consequently, she has a very original view! Guyon saw Revelation as a record of the believer's soul and what that soul must pass through to be transformed. All the beasts, dragons, plagues etc. are forces that launch themselves against the truly pious Christian (that is, the Christian following what Guyon calls "the inward way").

Guyon explains these assaults as experiences the soul

must pass through on its way to total transformation. As the soul passes through these dangers and catastrophes it is purified. These plagues of Revelation, she says, may be terrible, originating from evil men and dark forces, but nonetheless necessary – and allowed by God – for the sake of dealing with and changing the believer's soul.

We are not far from the facts when we say that Guyon simply used the drama of Revelation as a conveyance to communicate to her readers her teachings about the passage of the soul on its long journey to maturity. We recommend you view this book in that manner; in so doing you may find edification. But if you come to this writing expecting to gain some new view of eschatology – or to buttress an old one – you will be totally disappointed.

To put it in another way, this book is not an interpretation of Revelation . . . not as we understand that term in our day. It is, rather, an almost allegorical pilgrimage of the Christian soul, with Revelation's drama as the setting. Read this book as a modern interpretational view of Revelation and you will find nothing. Read it to help you understand what may await you in the Christian walk in the way of suffering, persecution and transformation. Read to be edified, then you may find no disappointment at all.

(If you want a capsulation or summation you will find one in Revelation, Chapter 17.)

Guyon wrote this book under excellent conditions to write on Revelation. She wrote it while fleeing persecution that came from her own church, originating specifically from the hands of church leaders who saw themselves as very pious Christians, walking properly in the way of the holiest saints of bygone days . . . and persecuting Guyon because she was not walking as they were. Jeanne Guyon, on the other hand, knew full well that these people were not truly godly. They opposed the godly and "the inward way" . . . and they – and their kind – had persecuted the Lord's most holy people in every age. Nor did this courageous lady mince words in saying so!

But just how accurate is her approach to Revelation? Scholars will find the answer to that question easy. She was utterly off base! She is often simplistic. Her interpretations often have no bearing on what we perceive as the obvious meaning of a passage. At other times her words are so unique they are refreshing.

But is she correct? Well, if we submit her book, and all the other books on Revelation – that are published this year – laying them all before learned theological scholars . . . her book will very definitely come in last!

But what if we submitted this same group of books to a gathering of first and second century believers?

We might get a shock. We might be told in definite and certain words that the modern-day interpretations of Revelation are almost totally void of the issue of the spiritual state of the Christian. We might also be shocked as we are told that our present interpretation of Revelation is almost totally materialistic in its underlying emphasis.

After all, first and second century believers really were not interested in what was happening in Russia, China, Britain, etc., etc. Most likely they had never heard of such places, and certainly didn't see them in Revelation, of all places! Rather, they might catch, in reading these present day books, an unspoken theme of: "Read my book and find out how to save your skin during the coming disaster". It is true, after all, that men today trade stocks, buy gold, store food and purchase cabins in northern Alaska based on the most recent insight into Revelation and the morning's news.

Let us not blame Revelation for this state of affairs. Nor present day authors. Their views reflect our prevailing Christian mind-set which is, essentially, Christian materialism.

In the 1790's when preachers of the British Isles, sons of a sophisticated, self-centered, provincial, protectionistic and materialistic society, saw their empire threatened by anarchy, when they saw their secure society crumbling, their traditional institutions flaunted, their caste system being undermined, they saw Revelation as a blueprint of Britain's future. (Just Britain's!) Be it ever so dire, here was a book telling the English their future. That same spirit is found in today's books on Revelation. The deeper Christian life does not even get consideration – not addressed, nor even dreamed of – as interpreters approach that mysterious book, pen in hand.

But how did the early Christian see Revelation? Quite differently! He saw himself as one walking in Christ, in the depths of Christ, even walking in spiritual realms. He saw the Christians he gathered with, first and foremost, as those who loved the Lord — experientially — and with a passion! Together they knew Him in the realm of the spirituals . . . not by accumulated head knowledge about Him.

When those pious believers read Revelation they saw an assault on the depth of their walk with Christ, that assault coming from forces utterly blind to what they really were.

After plowing through all the books about Revelation which will be printed this year, there is no question that Guyon's book would make more sense to a group of first and second century Christians than all the other books combined! For them, her book would come in first! Furthermore, you might make this test. The acid test. If you could choose any book on Revelation in print today — but only one book — which book would you pick to share a dungeon with?

But we must ask the question again. Just how accurate is Guyon's commentary on Revelation?

You be the judge.

REVELATION

1

Rev. 1:5,6: ... and from Jesus Christ, the faithful witness, the first born of the dead, and the ruler of the kings of the earth. To Him who loves us, and released us from our sins by His blood, and He has made us to be a kingdom, priests to His God and Father; to Him be the glory and the dominion forever and ever. Amen.

Everything is given to us through Jesus Christ for it is only by Him can anything be given.

Lord, You are the faithful witness; You have signed Your testimony with Your blood. And what is that testimony? You have established, between God and man, the testimony of reconciliation, and formed an alliance with human nature. In the presence of such a witness, we can be sure of Your love for mankind. You have given Yourself on the cross as a pledge of that love. You have kept the promises You have given us with an unbroken faithfulness. We see You standing before John, and before us, and we declare we doubt You not, oh Faithful Witness.

Jesus Christ was the first born in the bosom of death. He found immortality springing from the tomb. That tomb became the cradle of a life that can never be lost. In this unique birth, life out of death, He communicates life to all those who are fortunate enough to follow Him. Having life in Himself, He communicates it to others and, in so doing, withdraws them from death.

See Him, the King of kings. Through Him, and in Him, they (and we) all reign. All dominion is in Him alone.

Mankind must then acknowledge Your power and submit to it, giving You power over their lives.

Oh Jesus, You have loved us beyond all measure, in giving Yourself to death to raise us from the dead, delivering us from a second death.

And the dead ones mentioned here were filled with the corruption of their sins, yet You washed them in Your blood, opening thus an abundant fountain sufficient for all.

Rev. 1:7: Behold, He is coming with the clouds, and every eye will see Him, even those who pierced Him; and all the tribes of the earth will mourn over Him. Even so. Amen.

The Scriptures rightly say, "Behold," because the Lord's coming to you is a present happening. He comes, oh man, to knock at your heart. Do you not want to receive Him? Yes, He comes; to you! But the happy, fortunate day is nearer than we think, when the Bridegroom of our souls comes. Nothing is more certain! And how do You come, oh God? On the clouds? In the sacred darkness of faith? Every eye (that is to say, every understanding heart) will discover Him. That heart can see Him in those dark clouds—clouds in which He chooses to hide Himself.

The time is coming when every redeemed man will become "an inward being" and will embrace this light of faith ... believe in Him, adore Him in spirit and truth ... perhaps even those who pierced Him. Yes, those, the greatest sinners, the gentiles, and the Jews. Then every eye will see Him. All will believe in Him, all will worship Him; all will submit to Him. Then all the tribes of the earth, without exception, will shout for joy. He will become the admiration, the joy and wonder of all men. In that day, all will delight themselves in the Lord.

But before these times, oh God, how many crosses, persecutions, changes!

You alone know, Lord Jesus.

Rev. 1:8: "I am the Alpha and the Omega," says the Lord God, "who is and who was and who is to come, the Almighty."

The Word is the beginning and the end.

He is the beginning of all things, because all has been made by Him. But He wants to be something else also; He wishes to be in us, to be the beginning of all our works. He is in us, the beginning of all works. One day all men will know this simple fact . . . and will let Him move and direct their life, and give Life — and be their life. He comes to give all men His unique life, to turn them inward. As soon as He is the start of our actions, He becomes also their end; when we do all by Him, we do all for Him. This is the whole desire of Jesus Christ now. He desires to be the beginning and ending of all His creatures. Of you. For to the Word belongs the beginning — all beginnings — and end — and the ending — of all things. His Father gave Him all power and put all in His hands. All has been made by the Lord Jesus. Nothing was made without Him.

This is true, also, of the inner life. We begin by Jesus Christ and, wonder of wonders, we end by Him. After the believer has been hidden in God with Him, He is born in that believer, and lives and works in that one until He submerges him in the bosom of God. This is the Lord Who is, the Lord Who will always be, and the Lord Who comes into us — into you — in a special way.

> **Rev. 1:9: I, John, your brother and fellow partaker in the tribulation and kingdom and perseverance which are in Jesus, was on the island called Patmos, because of the word of the Lord and the testimony of Jesus.**

John is, of all apostles, the deepest . . . inwardly. He seemed to know, inwardly, what was given to each of us. John partook of the sufferings and afflictions of Jesus Christ. He, alone, accompanied Him to Calvary with unfailing loyalty. John shared His patience, suffering persecution, and bore with the weak believers (that is, all of us) in a gentle, loving, unusual way. This great Apostle did not rest till he was filled with love. What fire and flame he must have seen burning in his master's heart . . . and what fiery love then came to dwell in his own.

Yet, this man was persecuted. We must not be surprised to be persecuted for the same thing; on the contrary, we must rejoice.

Rev. 1:13: ... and in the middle of the lampstands one like a son of man, clothed in a robe reaching to the feet, and girded across His breast with a golden girdle.

The long garment covering the Lord Jesus is His purity and innocence; and the golden girdle is His love.

Rev. 1:14: And His head and His hair were white like white wool, like snow; and His eyes were like a flame of fire; ...

The Lord's head, here, represents His upper part, the whiteness of which shows His extreme integrity. His hair also was very white, signifying two things: the simplicity and purity of His thoughts, and His antiquity, since He was eternal as God, even though He had come in time as man. His eyes are as flames of fire. You see, the Word imparts the knowledge of the Father. This makes us understand that He is not present only to enlighten us but also to warm us with His love.

Rev. 1:15: ... and His feet were like burnished bronze, when it has been caused to glow in a furnace, and his voice was like the sound of many waters.

His feet stand for His humanity. His feet are fire standing in the furnace of divinity. Here is divine love for this, His earthly people. "His voice is as the sound of many waters," because His voice—in us—is the Word and is the strongest and deepest grace.

All graces that come to us and are granted to us are watered, immersed and made fruitful in us by means of a voice that is as mighty waters.

Rev. 1:17: And when I saw Him, I fell at His feet as a dead man. And He laid His right hand upon me, saying, "Do not be afraid; I am the first and the last, ..."

Now He appears as He truly is, to a man!
Oh Lord, as soon as You appear, truly man must fall as

dead. All that you and I have, which we received from Adam, has no strength! This "Adam" must die, so that the new Adam may do His work. But do not be afraid, for – by the touch of His right hand – He sustains the fallen believer and when he seems to be on the verge of perishing . . . there, in the midst of loss and death, he finds a greater salvation, a stronger life, a surer help. "Do not fear," says your Lord to you, "because I am the first and the last."

He says to you, "Indeed, I am the first to be found as soon as you enter in My way . . . I am the last to complete My work with you. It is as the First that I met you. You lost sight of me for a time. Now I am here again. The first meeting and the second are similar, yet different. Your second sight of Me is greater, and far better, than the first."

> **Rev. 1:18: ". . . and the living One; and I was dead, and behold, I am alive forevermore, and I have the keys of death and of Hades."**

Oh Word of God, You have life in Yourself and all live by You. Yet, though You are our very life and came to give life to men, You did not hesitate to suffer death willingly. You were immortal by nature, yet were willing to take on the form of a mortal body to destroy death. Ah, here is Your immense love and charity . . . submitting Yourself to death. Oh Essential Life, Your love made You find the way to submit to death and thereby free men from the certainty of death. You destroyed death with Your own death. It seemed, for a moment, that You allowed death to devour You; but You destroyed death. Now, death, through Your death, has produced Life! Death died! Now your Savior holds in His hands the keys of death and hell.

Oh Love, if You close, who can open? If You open, who can close? Open and close as You wish. But, the believer who puts his trust in You has such a special advantage: No one can enter hell unless You open hell's door; and You will never open it for that one who comes to Your open arms trustingly.

> **Rev. 1:19: "Write therefore the things which you have seen, and the things which are, and the things which shall take place after these things."**

John has received the command to write all that he has seen and will see. We can place Revelation at the level of the Gospels since in it we find Jesus Christ. We find Him as He is after His resurrection, ascension, and enthronement.

The faithful saints are the church, in perfect union; they are like a fire, a pure golden candlestick. That is, they are united in love, burning with the same fire as their Lord and enlightened with the same light.

2

Rev. 2:1–4: "To the angel of the church in Ephesus write:
The One who holds the seven stars in His right hand, the One who walks among the seven golden lampstands, says this: 'I know your deeds and your toil and perseverance, and that you cannot endure evil men, and you put to the test those who call themselves apostles, and they are not, and you found them to be false; and you have perseverance and have endured for My name's sake, and have not grown weary. But I have this against you, that you have left your first love.'"

This whole passage of Revelation points to the faithfulness of God. He, in turn, requires faithfulness in His followers. See the purity of God and the impurity of the creature, and how His penetrating light finds defects even in the angels. You who are called of God into His service, please note: God will not ask you for an exact account of your virtues in any way to be compared to His measure of your love for the flock. What faithfulness – a faithfulness in loving Him – He expects from the soul; know that His divine light would find darkness and impurity even in the sun!

There is none so virtuous as this church. However, the Lord reproves her for one thing. She is weakened in her first love. It seems to me that there is not a Christian who does not deserve this blame! Where are those who have kept themselves in their first fervor? Alas, where are they? How rare they are! Only at first do we show fervency and love;

after a while we respond to life's troubles with cowardliness.

Dear one, never take, as examples of love and fervor, the eagerness and desires of beginners, which often are very imperfect.

Your love must have a firm faithfulness to always do the will of God without getting tired of it, without leaving your consecration . . . in spite of hardships, dangers, fears, and persecutions.

> **Rev. 2:7: "'He who has an ear, let him hear what the Spirit says to the churches. To him who over-comes, I will grant to eat of the tree of life, which is in the Paradise of God.'"**

Our God is seen here as the victory, the conqueror.

No one can overcome but by You. You are, oh Jesus, this Lamb victorious over Satan and the flesh. And no one can overcome but in You and through You. But he who will con-quer in You, will do so by the loss of self; this one will eat of the fruit of the tree of life. You will give that Tree to him. And what is this fruit of life? It is Yourself, oh Jesus! Inwardly You feed the believer who receives You as life. As the believer gets lost in You, You quicken him, becoming his very life, his food.

> **Rev. 2:8, 9, 10: "And to the angel of the church in Smyrna write: The first and the last, who was dead, and has come to life, says this: 'I know your tribula-tion and your poverty (but you are rich), and the blasphemy by those who say they are Jews and are not, but are a synagogue of Satan. Do not fear what you are about to suffer. Behold, the devil is about to cast some of you into prison, that you may be tested, and you will have tribulation ten days. Be faithful until death, and I will give you the crown of life.'"**

This Jesus Christ is the first and the last. He is in the bosom of the Father, yet He became the least of men. He was dead but He is alive. Thus, those people who partake of death will partake of His life. Oh, men who are afflicted, in death, think! He who died for you (and like you), is alive for you. His life is in you. Eat of that Tree, partake of that life in you ... and you will live by Him – and you will live as He does!

Is there anything more comforting for a poor afflicted follower of Christ?

"I know your tribulation," says your Lord. "I know it." Is that not the greatest comfort?

I know your poverty, but you are rich.

What does this statement mean? It means that the greatest riches are found in the greatest poverty. A man who being deprived of all goods does not wish them. He finds in his bereavement an extreme satisfaction. Without any other stay, this follower of Christ trusts in God so much that he has no ground for his trust! He, therefore, possesses a treasure and vast riches. A wealthy man can desire for something, not being satisfied with his wealth. But the poor Christian just mentioned, being perfectly satisfied, has no need for anything. Having no need, he is perfectly rich!

But these people who are so at peace and satisfied are not known. God hides them in His sanctuary. He hides them from other eyes and even from their own eyes. Their holiness will be known only in eternity. They are slandered and condemned by all in this life. And by whom are they thus persecuted?

"By them which say they are Jews and are not." Whatever does this mean?

By those who are said to be pious, their piety consisting of outward forms and setting themselves against the lowly and spiritual ones.

The dear forsaken ones, living deep within the sanctuary of their spirits ... the true children of Abraham, and the true children of faith, do not fear what they must suffer.

This state is an advantage to you.

You will be persecuted even by saints, because they will have faith in slanders; but fear nothing. Darkness knows that its kingdom is more and more destroyed by the followers of Christ who aim at allowing God to reign in them, and aim at having Him reign in others. The kingdom of darkness raises against these strange persecutions. The dearest to God will find themselves in prison. Judges will be blinded ... the most innocent will appear guilty and the most devoted to the church, seen as enemies of her.

Fear not, it is but a trial.

"Ye shall have tribulation ten days."

How long is ten days? As long as your Lord deems that persecution must last. So, be faithful till death, if need be. For the interest of God, be faithful even to death. And in dying, do not lose faith and confidence. Your death will be crowned with everlasting life.

Rev. 2:11: 'He who has an ear, let him hear what the Spirit says to the churches. He who overcomes shall not be hurt by the second death.'

Two deaths have to be met, an internal, spiritual . . . and the more natural death. Only by the first do we overcome. This death allows Jesus Christ to conquer in us. He who is fortunate enough to overcome by this first death will not suffer the torments of the second death. That is, the second death is for him a pleasure, a refreshing. It is not said that these do not die, but only that they will not be hurt by the second death. This death is simply a passage from death to life.

Rev. 2:12–15: "And to the angel of the church in Pergamum write: The One who has the sharp two-edged sword says this: 'I know where you dwell, where Satan's throne is; and you hold fast My name, and did not deny My faith, even in the days of Antipas, My witness, My faithful one, who was killed among you, where Satan dwells. But I have a few things against you, because you have there some who hold the teaching of Balaam, who kept teaching Balak to put a stumbling block before the sons of Israel, to eat things sacrificed to idols, and to commit acts of immorality. Thus you also have some who in the same way hold the teaching of the Nicolaitans.' "

Please note that your Lord takes a name fitting the state of the persons whom He addresses. To those who are in affliction or in death, He shows them He was dead and He is alive. Why? So that he may give them the hope of a higher plane of life after having suffered a cruel death.

Now . . . to this group of believers . . . who have allowed

heresy, tolerating it, and suffering with it, He only speaks of His sword. This sword, the Word, destroys heresy.

"I know that for you, your faith is good, that you have kept it, being in fear when those of your faith were put to death. However, that cannot please Me, since you suffer Satan to share the ministry of the Church, tolerating a mixture which is offensive to Me. Oh God, You are extremely tender! Speak! You are the Word.

> **Rev. 2:16–17: 'Repent therefore; or else I am coming to you quickly, and I will make war against them with the sword of My mouth. He who has an ear, let him hear what the Spirit says to the churches. To him who overcomes, to him I will give some of the hidden manna, and I will give him a white stone, and a new name written on the stone which no one knows but he who receives it.'**

Oh Lord, You give the overcomer the hidden manna. And what is this hidden manna but Yourself? It is the intimate, secret, inward and unknown possession of Yourself. This manna is hidden in the sacred darkness of faith. Oh Word, so mysterious yet so real!

You give also to those who overcome . . . Your white stone. This is simply divine stillness. The believer is established in a most exquisite grace.

There is also a new name given to this one. The name is engraved on this white stone. The stone speaks of quietness and the whiteness of purity; the name shows the new life in God . . . and that name is engraved there. This name was given to Abraham, father of the believers and faithful souls, to Sarah, to Israel, and, in the New Testament, to Peter and to Paul. It is a name which none other than God Himself can give, since no other but He can place one in this state. Oh, great and wonderful state! Who will understand this? Only he who experiences it.

> **Rev. 2:18–19: "And to the angel of the church in Thyatira write: The Son of God, who has eyes like a flame of fire, and His feet are like burnished bronze, says this: 'I know your deeds, and your love and faith and service and perseverance, and that your deeds of late are greater than at first.'"**

My God, what wonderful expressions are in this book! The fire from the Lord's eyes shows the unsurpassed love He has for men (the eyes also represent all His knowledge of His Father). The feet like brass indicate His humanity which, joined to the Divinity, produced such great fires that they could have set ablaze a million worlds. However, where are those who will allow themselves to be filled, to be glowing in the flames? Alas, we all are like ice near such a blazing volcano.

The similarity of the qualities a person has, and the qualities which Jesus takes when with that one, is wonderful. So here, too, to a church. Here is a group of believers great in burning love. He places Love before her eyes, not so much to encourage them in such an unparalleled love, but to have them realize that – if they have such love – their Savior has infinitely more for them. But for what does He commend this people? For their works! Love, a work? They are alive with a perfect love and a living faith. He commends first their faith because the measure of faith is the measure of all graces, and the true measure of all outward and inward progress.

(According to your faith may it be done unto you, says Jesus Christ.)

He then commends their love. Faith and love go hand in hand. Where there is not much faith there is not much love, and where much love is, there is much faith. Love must not be measured by a shallow eagerness and fervency, but by faith!

One may ask: How do we know this faith?

By being generally, continually and steadily detached from what is inward or outward. The most annoying states will not move you. You do not express. You do not suppress. No. Not at all. Rather, you are simply unaffected. This faith will be faithful and full of confidence even in its apparent loss. Behavior is unaltered even in the greatest disasters. By this can the strength of faith and the truth of love be recognized!

Now we see the church is commended for her patience in suffering wrongs and evils. You see, it is from faith and love that patience is born. But above all, this gathering of believers is commended for not slackening. Her last works have surpassed the first, her watchfulness having been stronger toward the end than at the start. Oh, where will we find such a body of believers? How rare they are! How rare their bishops.

> **Rev. 2:20–21: 'But I have this against you, that you tolerate the woman Jezebel, who calls herself a prophetess, and she teaches and leads My bond-servants astray, so that they commit acts of immorality and eat things sacrificed to idols. And I gave her time to repent; and she does not want to repent of her immorality.'**

Oh, pure Love, divine exacting One, from Your omniscience nothing can be hidden. What blame can You bring against such a pastor whom You commended so highly? Oh God, next to Your purity every other purity is impure! Oh, ministers of the flock of Jesus Christ, how terrible is your charge, and what an account you will have to give! It is not enough for you to be holy; you must see to it that others are holy also. God is not satisfied for you to banish all kinds of sin from your heart, if you do not also banish them from His Church and from the midst of His flock.

The wording of the Scriptures is praiseworthy; all is fornication and adultery which is opposed to God's honor, stealing the honor due to Him to give it to others. A fornication of the heart and an adultery of the mind is more dangerous – and·worse – than that of the body. Here you see the results of a heart and mind withdrawn from God . . . the God to whom they belong.

Who is this corrupt Jezebel? This unfortunate Jezebel represents the corrupted nature which takes away the mind from being attached to God ... and directs that mind toward unruly desires. In His desire to save a man, God arrests a wayward one with sicknesses. (This is often God's procedure.)

Your Lord declares that He "searches the reins and hearts." Oh Lord, judgment belongs to you. How blind we are of ourselves! We hide our true heart. With the finest excuses, we hide from our very own selves our real intentions. We act for ourselves, in self love, persuading ourselves – and others – that we are really acting for God alone.

However, God "will give every one according to your works." Works are not counted by their quantity but by the presence of grace, of goodness, of Christ ... deep within that man. That is why this gathering of believers is weighed in the balance and not accepted.

How many more will be thusly surprised!

Some who believe they have a great many works, will be without. And others, who have appeared useless, will have a heavy weight of good works. It is not the outward works themselves ... NO ... it is the amount of grace, the extent of Christ, in the inward heart ... from which came that work! Oh God, how right You are to hold justice in Your hands!

> Rev. 2:26-28: 'And he who overcomes, and he who keeps My deeds until the end, to him I will give authority over the nations; and he shall rule them with a rod of iron, as the vessels of the potter are broken to pieces, as I also have received authority from My father; and I will give him the morning star.'

He who has overcome through dying inwardly (in whom all is destroyed) has a wonderful advantage reserved for him by God. In this band of believers the Lord Jesus alone reigns. Their souls have the faithfulness to give Him all the glory of the victory without claiming anything for themselves. This is right indeed since He alone is victorious in us. The victory is there. They have not prevented the victory. These, who did not prevent this victory – because they have let everything go to be destroyed – all these (but how rare,and how few, they are) will "have power over the nations."

They will have this power in several ways.

First, they will have a great authority over the souls of men and even over their persons.

Secondly, they will have power over themselves. Thirdly, after they are dead, God uses them to govern His Church. God takes them as Pastors. God wants those who have kept His will till the end ... then "will they govern them with a rod of iron." Why? Because their authority is so strong, nothing can oppose them. It is not a hard authority however! These believers, dead to love of self, have divine power. They handle things as they please, even the most inward and hidden things. As time goes by, they reveal that a divine power has been communicated to them. The Lord now adds something else: "I will give him the morning star." This morning star precedes dawn. The believer who "receives the morning star" has a right and an advantage given by God: He moves and He instructs in the true spirit of Jesus Christ. Your Lord is the morning star announcing a day in which the travelers may walk in the inward way.

3

Rev. 3:1,2: "And to the angel of the church in Sardis write: He who has the seven Spirits of God, and the seven stars, says this: 'I know your deeds, that you have a name that you are alive, but you are dead. Wake up, and strengthen the things that remain, which were about to die; for I have not found your deeds completed in the sight of My God.'"

How many churches, how many workers are there who are dead though they seem alive? And why are they dead? Because they have no strength or life. They are dead because all they do is not animated by the inner Spirit and by pure love. In all their actions they seek only a vain smoke of reputation.

"He who has the seven Spirits of God and the seven stars . . ." The seven Spirits of God is that divine light which discovers that which is most hidden. It is your Lord who discovers that you were dead though you seemed alive . . . alive to all . . . except to Him. "Be watchful" to come out of this death. How many gatherings of believers are there, like these. From them the wolf snatches the sheep! Ah, how many will be found with lukewarm works! There is more here. It seems some have become shepherds of the flock to eat the butter and drink the milk of their flock, to cover themselves with their wool, yet not to guard, defend and sustain that flock.

We are not surprised, then, at such death.

Rev. 3:4,5: 'But you have a few people in Sardis who have not soiled their garments; and they will walk with Me in white; for they are worthy. He who overcomes shall thus be clothed in white garments; and I will not erase his name from the book of life, and I will confess his name before My Father, and before His angels.'

There is no country, no city that is so corrupt but what we could find saintly persons there. Often the places with the most corruptions are those from which the greatest saints come. He that overcometh . . . is the one destroyed and dead, . . . he it is who is reinstated to the first grace, the state of innocence. God's grace in our redemption has brought man back to his first condition, with advantages that he did not even have previous to that redemption! Otherwise redemption would not equal creation, and thus redemption would not be abundant. We do not all enjoy the full extent of the benefit of redemption because we do not allow Jesus Christ to spread over us the graces of redemption and the result of all His merits. But those who overcome in Him, and by Him, partake of this fulness; that is why Revelation shows us that such ones are clothed in raiment that is white; they are clothed with the garments of redemptive innocence. Their name will never be blotted out of the book of life; Jesus Christ will confess them before the Father, recognizing them as His own. They will be received by Him as children of adoption, heirs of God and co-heirs with Jesus Christ.

Rev. 3:6: 'He who has an ear, let him hear what the Spirit says to the churches.'

Oh God, in this age in which we now live, the greatest truths are considered errors and blasphemies. Those who speak of the deepest of Thy ways are the target of hatred and of men's opposition. Crimes, foolishness and filth are well thought of; those who speak of them and do them are said to be honest, while Your servants, oh Lord, are shamefully thought of. It seems, my God, that You are blind and do not see what is taking place. You see them, Lord, and protect these adversaries so as to try Your servants' patience and thereby refine them; You reserve the opposers for the day of Your wrath.

> **Rev. 3:7,8,9: "And to the angel of the church in Philadelphia write: He who is holy, who is true, who has the key of David, who opens and no one will shut, and who shuts and no one opens, says this: 'I know your deeds. Behold, I have put before you an open door which no one can shut, because you have a little power, and have kept My word, and have not denied My name. Behold, I will cause those of the synagogue of Satan, who say that they are Jews, and are not, but lie — behold, I will make them to come and bow down at your feet, and to know that I have loved you.'"**

This gathering of believers is the only one to whom no rebuke is given. They have "a little strength." This is because God strengthened them, and, having no strength in themselves, they put their strength in God.

What qualities does Jesus assume for them? They are "holy" and "true," completely brought to nought; their entire holiness is in God. Jesus is holy for them. They are called "true" because they have been placed in the truth; and though they do not receive as many praises as some others, these two qualities which Jesus has assumed for them contain all other graces. They are not blamed for anything, simply because, in weakness, they have found His strength. Having no self interest, their only interest is that of God. They only wish the extension of His kingdom and souls.

"I will make them to come and worship at your feet." Others will discover, by experience, what they will receive by coming to these blessed believers. They will discover this, "that I have loved you!"

This holy and true God tells His servant, "I have the key of David." "He opens and no one will shut and shuts and no one opens." What is this opening? It is that of His Father's bosom. If He does not open this bosom, no one will enter, for no one can open it but He Himself. But once it is opened, nothing in the world can close it again. This door — He opened it to His servants to usher them in and hide them with Him. There, these servants will be made conquerors over and over again.

> **Rev. 3:10:** '**Because you have kept the word of My perseverance [patience], I also will keep you from the hour of testing, that hour which is about to come upon the whole world, to test those who dwell upon the earth.**'

To keep the Word of His patience means to suffer inwardly and outwardly in everything that comes, considering this the will of God. When we have suffered in this manner, there is still another way to keep the Word of His patience: to remain silent and keep still. To be still for a long time after God has spoken to the soul, and after He has loaded that soul with blessings. The believer then keeps the Word of His patience, for just as God waited for that One a long time, the believer waits also for Him a long time; and persevering in patience, keeps His Word, doing His whole will. How well kept is a soul kept in this manner! When nearly all yield to temptation, he is kept from it.

There are two temptations: that of pleasure and that of grief. Men have been so corrupted for centuries, that they do all to corrupt the saints. The temptation of pleasure has been used against even martyrs. Some can resist suffering but can not resist pleasure. God permits both, to test and purify those who belong to Him, allowing them to despise both! The lives of the holy believers who have come before us give many examples of these two temptations. Today we see God's servants persecuted, afflicted, despised of men. It seems they are as the dung of the earth. Alas, so few are those who are faithful in temptation. Everyone wants to please, to receive credit; all are full of ambition. Few worry about pleasing God or being esteemed by Him . . . it is only that they please men and are esteemed of men. They appreciate a virtue esteemed by the world, and do not want the virtue of Jesus Christ. However, God's true servants who suffer offences without complaining and slanders without justifying themselves are specially protected in the day of temptation . . . so says the Scripture.

> **Rev. 3:11,12:** '**I am coming quickly; hold fast what you have, in order that no one take your crown. He**

who overcomes, I will make him a pillar in the temple of My God, and he will not go out from it anymore; and I will write upon him the name of My God, and the name of the city of My God, the new Jerusalem, which comes down out of heaven from My God, and My new name.'

What wonderful mysteries! Jesus Christ assures this church that He is coming soon.

Today He calls out, to Himself, those fellowshipping with Him—within—drawing them from the world . . . which is unworthy of them.

"Hold fast what you have." This can be understood in two ways: We should not, through our fault, come down from the state in which God has lifted us through His kindness, but we should persevere till the end. Secondly, we see the believer realizing his nothingness (for that is all he owns) and he must remain thus. We must remain in this state or the crown will be given to another, for the crown above all crowns is reserved for the state of nothingness.

"He who overcomes" will have the advantage of being a "pillar" in the church, an unmovable pillar because of its steadiness. These overcomers uphold the church, though they are not known as such. A firm column preventing the tottering of the building, yet unseen, undiscovered. My God, sustain Your church, thusly.

God places this believer in a divine stillness in Him, establishing him in Christ so that he will never leave. Oh blissful state for this soul, who will never more lose God. The name of God will be engraved on him, on his heart, as it was given the Bride in the Song of Songs when the Lord said to her: "Set me as a seal upon thine heart, as a seal upon thine arm." This name which is engraved on this person stands for an entire consecration without and within. Jesus Christ engraved also on him "the name of the city of her God." He does this in two ways, by joining him to the number of the holy believers and giving him all the features of holiness . . . the very name of the holy city in heaven. Second, by placing in this one all the features and character of the Church's purity. You could almost say the internal life of this believer is a miniature of the Church, a Church so purified and perfected that no inner or outward resemblance to Jesus Christ is left unexpressed in a group of such persons. All outward service for the overcomer is easy. These persons are kept, when they have become nothing, at the end of their days, to be the lights in the Church. All nations come to their fragrance to find their Lord.

He adds that He will engrave "the name of the new Jerusalem which comes down out of heaven.

What is this new Jerusalem? This can be nothing else except the Church. The Church is already formed and the Holy Spirit has come to fill her. Here we are told that this Spirit of the Church will be outpoured on all its members, and communicated to them. This Spirit is the Spirit of the divine moving which is the general Spirit of the Church. This Spirit is going to be outpoured very soon on all her members. As it is written: You will "all be taught of the Lord." How will they be taught? They will listen to the Lord, and hear Him . . . and become attentive to His voice. That is why the devil fights, with all his might, prayer and loving concentration to God.

This Holy Spirit comes from God to be outpoured on the creatures and Joel's prophetic word will be completely fulfilled. Although it was fulfilled when the Holy Spirit came on the whole Church through the assembled Apostles and the faithful, it was not however perfectly fulfilled, since this Holy Spirit was not outpoured on all flesh, though it came on men and women. But a time will come when this prophecy will have its full extension.

Elsewhere Jesus Christ says He will give the overcomers a new name. But here He says He will give "His new name." There is a wide difference between one expression and the other. The new name is given as soon as the believer loses his own identity through nothingness and is in God. But when Jesus Christ gives this one His new name, He gives him the name of the Lord. He will use this person for the salvation of many souls and will impart to that one His sufferings by crucifying that one with Him.

Rev. 3:13: 'He who has an ear, let him hear with the Spirit says to the churches.'

A deep wisdom is needed to understand this. If there were only a natural meaning hidden in these words, they would not be repeated so often. "He who has an ear, let him hear." But there is a mystical sense, so pointed and so deep that we must not be surprised it is so often repeated. Oh deep words, who will understand you!

> **Rev. 3:14,15,16: "And to the angel of the church in Laodicea write: The Amen, the faithful and true Witness, the Beginning of the creation of God, says this: 'I know your deeds, that you are neither cold nor hot; I would that you were cold or hot. So because you are lukewarm, and neither hot nor cold, I will spit you out of My mouth.'"**

However unruly a group of believers may be, they are part of His Church. Jesus Christ here gives Himself marvelous qualities. I am, He says, the Amen, the true being. There is nothing besides Me. I am essence. All other beings exist in Me and by Me. I am; and what is not Myself is nothing. Why this Amen? Because there is nothing to be added, for when Jesus Christ says: "I am that I am," this is all that can be positively said of Him.

He repeats He is the faithful and true witness and as He said it to him who did right, He says it to him who fails. For He is the faithful witness of righteousness. He is also the witness of evil, uncovering evil and recording it. That is why, being as exact as He is, it will be a terrible thing for us to fall in the hands of the living God. In order for this not to be so for us, we must put in His hands our whole life, acting only by His leadings and following His Spirit. Then all our works will be done with assurance; and He will be the faithful and true witness of them. He will not reject any of the works He has done Himself! Besides the literal sense that all creatures have been created by the Word and that all life springs from His, I say that all works, in order to come from God and be considered by Him as His works, must have this principle: that Jesus Christ must be the agent of them, that they are done under His Spirit, and done while in spirit. He must be the moving power of them.

The rebuke of Jesus Christ through John to this gathering is frightful. It is certain that there are no persons more opposed to receiving the true Spirit of God, the inner Spirit, than lukewarm Christians. The reason for this is that the carelessness with which they do all that pertains to God is so great that the little warmth that is left appears to them to be a great fire. They do not understand they do

24

evil, and the love they have for themselves makes them believe so strongly they are doing well, that they cannot doubt it!

All that is said to them to get them out of that state offends them! Such words make them see in others a blindness which is their own! A blindness it is which they do not wish to recognize or admit.

This evil is then without remedy! Further, it is nourished and established by self-sufficiency and self-love. They prefer themselves to sinners (whom they look upon with disdain and scorn). They prefer themselves, and their views, to the greatest saints of all time. They are opposed to receiving an effecting portion of the Spirit of God more than the greatest sinner is. That is why Jesus Christ says concerning the one spoken of here: "I would that you were cold." If he were cold he would be easily converted! He would be convinced of his coldness, and he would receive with humility the advice given him.

If not cold, then hot.

But because "he is neither cold nor hot, I will vomit him out of my mouth."

Oh, this is the most frightful word in the world! Once you are vomited, there is no more hope, for a thing you throw away can be picked up again, but a vomited thing is never again gathered. How these words should make any who are thus to tremble. Doing right only through routine is dangerous! Odd, is it not, that the lukewarm believe they are filled with warmth, while these filled with warmth, in some seasons, believe themselves to be lukewarm.

> **Rev. 3:17: 'Because you say, "I am rich, and have become wealthy, and have need of nothing," and you do not know that you are wretched and miserable and poor and blind and naked, . . .'**

What is most strange about lukewarm people is, they believe they are richer in graces than anyone else, and filled with spiritual goods. It seems to them that they need no one, and they believe that everyone else needs them. They invariably oblige everybody to accept their advice and their view. They believe themselves to be in a place in which they can advise all. They do not wish to be advised by anyone! While another gathering of believers in Asia Minor was apparently poor yet immensely rich, this group thinks itself rich while very "poor" in God and in His graces. Loving themselves, they are very wretched. They cannot be really glad; they lack everything since they lack what is essential – perfect love, abandonment to God, perfect giving up of each life, resignation, submission to God's Will, unselfishness, etc. They are "miserable" because though they appear outwardly glad, they are driven inwardly by the love of glory, the desire to be counted as somebody though they are nothing.

Let one of these be touched by contempt or the least affliction . . . and he will be overwhelmed completely. They are "poor and naked." Why? Because they are stripped of all – for being not clothed with Jesus Christ or animated by His Spirit, is to be poor and naked indeed. They are also blind, yet believing that they are all right.

Rev. 3:18: 'I advise you to buy from Me gold refined by fire, that you may become rich, and white garments, that you may clothe yourself, and that the shame of your nakedness may not be revealed; and eyesalve to anoint your eyes, that you may see.'

Oh Love, only You can impart the perfect love which is that "gold tried in the fire." Only You can place in our soul pure virtues. Only You can clothe us with this Spirit of faith which is a very pure gold. Only You can produce in us these works so perfect in love that fire cannot spoil them. To You then we must come "to buy this gold." But what do You want us to give You for its price? "Buy of Me," He says, "without money and without price." He requires nothing as a payment because He knows too well that we have nothing. He just wants us to give ourselves to Him, to abandon ourselves to Him without reserve. It is He Who also gives us white raiment, the robe of innocence and truthfulness with which He clothes His servants. This robe of innocence must cover that nakedness of human nature. Do not think this is impossible, for the grace of redemption must exceed the grace of creation, and that repaired innocence must be more abundant than the original innocence. Moreover, Jesus Christ, inviting us to go to Him, speaks of love and innocence in terms of wine and milk. As for love, He imparts it to us, by His Holy Spirit – an advantage which Adam never had.

He adds that He will put eyesalve on our eyes, so that we can see clearly. This eyesalve is simply the Spirit of faith which frees us from the blindness in which we are kept by our reasoning and our self-love. We shall know then that we are poor, whereas we thought we were rich; that we are naked whereas we thought we were covered more than all.

Rev. 3:19: 'Those whom I love, I reprove and discipline; be zealous therefore, and repent.'

The greatest proof of love that God can give us is that He warns us about our faults. As for those whom God does not love, He withholds their chastisement for the day of His wrath, but He corrects the least faults of those He loves. An "inner" believer has, within, a director reproving unceasingly, a master correcting and chastening continuously; it seems that God has nothing else to do but reprove and correct this soul. This is the greatest proof of His love.

Rev. 3:20: 'Behold, I stand at the door and knock; if anyone hears My voice and opens the door, I will come in to him, and will dine with him, and he with Me.'

Jesus Christ always stands at the door of our heart; He waits for us to open to Him. Oh Christians, whoever you may be, not opening your door to your Savior, are you not very ungrateful not to open your whole heart to God, He who opened His on the cross to receive you? At the very door of your heart He is knocking. There is not one of us, who paying attention to God within, would fail hearing His knock at the heart's door. But if you do not hear, it is because you do not pay attention. Get used to stilling your soul, they you will hear Him knocking at the door of your heart. As soon as you open, yielding yourself to Him unreservedly, He will enter. But how can we hear His voice if we do not listen?

Oh Love, You speak to the heart which has no ear to hear You because he is attentive to the voices of creation, about him. He is not attentive to You; he does not discern Your voice. If he would react against himself just a little to listen to Your voice, he would unmistakably hear it, and no sooner would he have heard, than You would come within. He would then sense Your divine presence in an unspeakable way – a way that would surprise him so because he was not expecting such a unique grace. But Jesus Christ would not stop there. He admits you to His banquet. With you who listen He shares His feast and love. Jesus Christ is your food, and gives Himself to you. Your Lord would have you taste the most delicious of all nourishment ... Jesus Christ – within! Oh Christians, you who are born for such great wealth which you can have if you only wish, shall you deprive yourself of it? We wrongly have in mind that this is a grace reserved for very few people and that it is almost impossible to obtain; however, everlasting truth assures us that there is nothing easier to have. Is there anything easier than opening a door to a person who unceasingly stands by it, knocking continuously? And what is easier than hearing Him Who always speaks so as to be obeyed? There is nothing easier. However, He does ask for an opening. He asks to be heard so as to come in to us, to be unceasingly present. He asks us to accept admission to His feast, and He asks "to sup with us" – that is, to share our troubles; and for us "to sup with Him" – that is, to share in His divine delights. You only have to stretch out your hand! Ah, blindness today is so great, be not part of it.

> **Rev. 3:21,22: 'He who overcomes, I will grant to him to sit down with Me on My throne, as I also overcame and sat down with My Father on His throne. He who has an ear, let him hear what the Spirit says to the churches.'**

The throne of Jesus Christ is nothing less than the bosom of the Father. The throne is given Him eternally. His humanity has been favored by His divinity through His death, and through the victory He won over hell and self. The throne is His. "He who overcomes" through Jesus Christ, will be received in God with Him and will share this throne. "He who has an ear" to listen "let him hear" these things and understand the kindnesses and mercies of God for His dear creation.

4

Rev. 4:1: After these things I looked, and behold, a door standing open in heaven, and the first voice which I had heard, like the sound of a trumpet speaking with me, said, "Come up here, and I will show you what must take place after these things."

Jesus Christ opens the door of heaven to that one who will open his heart to Him. A time will come in the future when the heart of man will be opened to Him and to His voice. Oh God, as much as Your inner ways are spoken evil of and despised in this hour, so much will they be esteemed and followed in future centuries.*

Rev. 4:2,3: Immediately I was in the Spirit; and behold, a throne was standing in heaven, and One sitting on the throne. And He who was sitting was like a jasper stone and a sardius in appearance; and there was a rainbow around the throne, like an emerald in appearance.

This is the throne of God and the brightness of His majesty. Jesus Christ shows John this to give some pledge of the glory He has prepared for His elect ones and to give John some idea of the fearful greatness of God. God is seated on this throne because His rest is never interrupted. His throne is immense, and can only be filled by Him. The

---

*Lord, we are still waiting.

color "like a jasper and a sardius stone" shows its stillness, its immutability, and the steadfastness and duration of His glory. This circle of emerald signifies peace and reconciliation, and this is witnessed by the rainbow. The color of this rainbow is emerald, to show that reconciliation is in our Savior Jesus Christ alone, and that no one will be saved and enjoy the advantage of this reconciliation except by their hope in this divine Savior. This rainbow surrounds God, which indicates that the humanity of Jesus Christ surrounds the divinity within Him.

> Rev. 4:4,5: And around the throne were twenty-four thrones; and upon the thrones I saw twenty-four elders sitting, clothed in white garments, and golden crowns on their heads. And from the throne proceeded flashes of lightning and sounds and peals of thunder. And there were seven lamps of fire burning before the throne, which are the seven Spirits of God; . . .

These twenty-four elders are the holy Patriarchs and Prophets, the most faithful, and most beloved of God. They were, so to speak, the foundation for all the other saints who follow. God showed these elders to John to have him understand the glory He reserves for those He admits to His banquet.

On these wonderful thrones the Son of man will place those who overcome in Him and by Him!

These thrones are reserved for those who leave all to follow Him. "Ye which have followed Me . . . .ye shall also sit upon twelve thrones."

These elders are also dressed in white; they had been reinstated in their innocence by the grace of Jesus Christ, given to them in its fullness after His death. They have been crowned with perfect love.

Oh God, who is man whom You should honor with so many graces and such glory?

But oh, foolish and insane man, losing divine and eternal delights for a moment's pleasure which is not even worthy of being called pleasure. Oh, ambitious ones, wanting to be kings in this world, aspire rather to be kings in heaven! These on the throne have been brought to nothing. That is why you surround the throne of the One who became nothing, taking the form of servant and slave. The measure of nothingness is the measure of glory.

This reign that Jesus Christ possesses in the throne of David and in the throne of God will have no end. The high degree of glory to which David has been raised can be understood by the deep humiliations to which he was reduced. So, thus, with the Son of David. Those who are fortunate enough to have a part in the humiliation of these saints will have a share in their glory.

The holy ones of past ages are sanctified looking forward to the blood of Jesus Christ which was to be shed or had been shed. We, by looking back. In this century (where wickedness is at its height), holy ones will still come into being, by means of a God Who takes pleasure in producing holy ones in all ages. The world would perish without these saints! God puts up with the ungodly on account of the righteous.

There are "seven Spirits of God" full of lights and flames, like lamps which are always lit, to honor His supreme greatness.

"And out of the throne proceeded lightnings and thunderings and voices."

This shows the majesty, greatness, and dignity of God. Moses once saw the majesty of God and exclaimed, "You are wonderful, terrible, and merciful," adding many spontaneous words to explain what he saw, but which explained very little what he meant. So John, too, exclaims, but little is explained; such is a view of God's majesty.

> Rev. 4:6,7: . . . and before the throne there was, as it were, a sea of glass like crystal; and in the center and around the throne, four living creatures full of eyes in front and behind. And the first creature was like a lion, and the second creature like a calf, and the third creature had a face like that of a man, and the fourth creature was like a flying eagle.

"The four living creatures, full of eyes" are filled with the knowledge of Jesus Christ, with what He said and did, so as to let us all know. The lion is like the state of the saints who defended the Church. The calf defends His church, also. This was the time when saints roared. The man is as the saints who imitate Christ outwardly. The fourth is an eagle flying above the others. This represents those to whom the inner Spirit, the Spirit of Jesus Christ, is imparted.

All things will become inwardly understood. We do not mean to say that the martyrs were not inward souls. However, each was excellent in his particular quality. They are "full of eyes" because they are full of light and knowledge.

Nonetheless, of the four, the eagle flies above the others.

John is given the eagle because he flew higher than anyone.

As we read the Gospel of John we see that he takes us to the very bosom of God and draws from Jesus Christ, discovering through his humanity the advantages of his Divinity; John it is who searches what is deepest in Jesus Christ. It is certain that times are coming when purer lights than those which exist today are going to be uncovered for the Church. There will not be anything earthly in this ministry; all will be spiritual and divine. Men will seem to be dwelling near the Sun, as the eagle does, through the pure lights which will be given to them.

These living creatures tell us something; they reveal different stages which believers must pass through to reach the throne. The first creature is filled with fire, strength, and courage, like a lion. The second has much of the animal or the beast. (David expressed this when he said: "I was as a beast before thee"). When men lose this brutish state they become fully human, having nothing left as far as courage or stupidity is concerned; the life of divine humanity comes through the cross and the woes of this life. But finally the believer becomes as an eagle. Just as he was linked to earth, so now he is detached from it. This last state of the believer withdraws wholly from the previous three.

> Rev. 4:8: And the four living creatures, each one of them having six wings, are full of eyes around and within; and day and night they do not cease to say,
> "Holy, holy, holy is the Lord God, the Almighty,
> who was and who is and who is to come."

The six wings of these living creatures carry them. They have eyes without and within representing their outward and inward enlightening. All is light with them. They discover and penetrate everything. "They rest not day and night." They sing just the same in the day of joy and in the darkness of afflictions, in the inner light and in a dark state. "They say, Holy, Holy, Holy" because God is holy ... day or night! They understand that holiness is wholly in God. They are near the throne to give Him the glory which is due Him on account of His holiness.

"You only are holy. We do not recognize any other holiness but Yours."

But why do you shout so?

"Because of the light we have that God alone is holy, and we wish that everybody should know Him in such a way." These four living creatures cry out without ceasing that He is "Almighty" ... not only holy, but He can make us holy. "He was, is and is to come." There is nothing that is truly real and lasting but Him.

Oh God, if we could only give You a glory as infinite as You are infinite! But as this is not possible, may these creatures which You uphold and which behold You give You all the glory they can give. And may we join them!

> Rev. 4: 9,10,11: And when the living creatures give glory and honor and thanks to Him who sits on the throne, to Him who lives forever and ever, the twenty-four elders will fall down before Him who sits on the throne, and will worship Him who lives forever and ever, and will cast their crowns before the throne, saying,
>
> "Worthy art Thou, our Lord and our God, to receive
> glory and honor and power; for Thou didst create all
> things, and because of Thy will they existed, and
> were created."

All saints owe Him much glory and gratefulness; from Him is all the glory of their holiness. He is their purifier and He has given Himself for them; He has sanctified them by His blood. They can never acknowledge too much such an excessive mercy.

Now we see "the twenty-four elders" (the most humble

and nearest to God) "fall down before Him." Their falling down bodily shows how they brought to nought themselves so as to allow Him to be all in them. They seem to give this eternal knowledge to all future ages: The manner of honoring God as God is through nothingness. They now do in heaven what they had done on earth. "They cast their crowns before Him," to show that they have made Him their king, allowing Him to reign in them and over them, ceasing to govern themselves or to lead themselves. They have yielded to Him all the rights they had over themselves. They show He reigns in them perfectly, that they have been His kingdom as He has been their king. They glorify Him through nothingness, and by yielding to Him.

They now cry out to God: "You are worthy, O Lord, to receive glory and honor and power." No one is more worthy than You. You are infinitely glorified in Yourself, and You must be so in Your creation.

"For You have created all things." All is done in His divine will. When the soul is left without any will of its own, it begins to enter into a new state and into a new creation.

5

Rev. 5:1: And I saw in the right hand of Him who sat on the throne a book written inside and on the back, sealed up with seven seals.

This little book, what is its content? This book shows only Jesus Christ, the God man. It is written inside and out with the truth of God, which He came to bring to the world. Without Him this truth would not be known. Within, as the Word, He is the truth of God. Without, He is the truth that all men must read because He is the truth they must become the image of. Truth has always been hidden in God.

This book is "in the right hand of God," because the Word, as is the right hand, is the whole power of God. "All power is given Him in heaven and earth." In heaven power is given Him to express all the truth of God; on earth, power is given Him to show a little of this truth to men. As John has said, "They saw Him, the fullness of grace and truth."

This book is "sealed with seven seals." Before truth, in its fullness, can be set within us, we must pass through seven deepenings of the Holy Spirit.

Rev. 5:2,3: And I saw a strong angel proclaiming with a loud voice, "Who is worthy to open the book and to break its seals?" And no one in heaven, or on the earth, or under the earth, was able to open the book, or to look into it.

There is discovered no one in heaven, not even the angels, or the greatest of the holy ones, who can open this book. Opening this book is really opening the bosom the Lord.

Oh God in heaven, on earth, and under the earth, who is even worthy to do so? Who can discover Jesus Christ and His truth? Who can look at it except You, and thereby reveal what is hidden to us?

Rev. 5:4,5: And I began to weep greatly, because no one was found worthy to open the book, or to look into it; and one of the elders said to me, "Stop weeping; behold, the Lion that is from the tribe of Judah, the Root of David, has overcome so as to open the book and its seven seals."

John begins to cry. Why? That which caused his tears will be his greatest joy, because the joy of a loving heart is to know that all power is in God. As soon as the mystery is discovered, he is filled with joy. (One of the elders comforts him and tells him not to weep because the strong and victorious Lion of the tribe of Judah, that immortal Root of David, has succeeded in opening this book.) The book is open on behalf of men, showing them this truth by His victory over falsehood. When men think the deepest truths of Christ have been destroyed, then its chains will be broken, prison doors open and it appears. To whom? To His own people, and with more brightness than ever, filling His followers with joy.

Rev. 5:6: And I saw between the throne (with the four living creatures) and the elders a Lamb standing, as if slain, having seven horns and seven eyes, which are the seven Spirits of God, sent out into all the earth.

In the middle of the throne, in the midst of God Himself, we discover the Lamb, slain for the sins of the world. This Lamb slain so as to wash the robes of men in His blood, to cover them with His wool, to nourish them with His very Life and Spirit, is in the midst of the living creatures and elders, because He is the happiness of all saints! He is the center of all saints!

The seven eyes are the lights of His Spirit which He

spreads everywhere and the seven horns are the abundance of His grace which He distributes to men.

Rev. 5:7,8: And He came, and He took it out of the right hand of Him who sat on the throne. And when He had taken the book, the four living creatures and the twenty-four elders fell down before the Lamb, having each one a harp, and golden bowls full of incense, which are the prayers of the saints.

The Lamb receives "the book from the hand of Him that sat upon the throne," for He has received all things from Him and now, what He received from the Father He imparts to men.

To express awe and gratefulness the elders and the living creatures fall down before the Lamb, for He is about to show truth on earth. He is taking truth from the bonds which hold it captive.

The harps are the praises and harmony of these holy ones ... and their oneness with the will of God.

"The golden vials the prayers of the saints."

Here you see the intercession of all the holy believers. These prayers are in golden vials, indicating they are offered with the purest perfume. True prayer is from a broken soul just as is the perfume coming out of burning incense.

Rev. 5:9: And they sang a new song, saying, "Worthy art Thou to take the book, and to break its seals; for Thou wast slain, and didst purchase for God with Thy blood men from evern tribe and tongue and people and nation."

The ones consumed by all they have seen cannot prevent themselves from singing "a new song," a very wonderful song known only to God and to the soul that sings it.

The song is of deliverance, joy, happiness and satisfaction. This song is only about God, for all interest in the creature has completely vanished. This song cannot be explained with words. They rejoice that He has opened this book of truth, broken its seals, and redeemed them and all men with the price of His blood ... redeemed them that they may belong wholly and only to God.

Rev. 5:10: "And Thou hast made them to be a kingdom and priests to our God; and they will reign upon the earth."

Believers who are dead to self-love become kings. They reign over themselves and all others. They have become priests giving unto God a continual sacrifice of praise. They reign not only in heaven but even on earth. Oh, could the ambitious rulers and would-be rulers possess this noble ambition of ruling!

Rev. 5:11,12: And I looked, and I heard the voice of many angels around the throne and the living creatures and the elders; and the number of them was myriads of myriads, and thousands of thousands, saying with a loud voice,
"Worthy is the Lamb that was slain to receive power and riches and wisdom and might and honor and glory and blessing."

The Angels are around the throne, the living creatures and the elders.
Oh God, You did not want only to love Yourself, but You wanted to be loved. That is the purpose of creation! Not only do You enable them to contemplate and to love You, but You contemplate Yourself in them and You place Your Word in them. This which we were created from, men say is the very thing they declare to be impossible.
The angels now speak "with a loud voice" so as to be heard by all. They want all the earth to know that this spotless Lamb, Who was slain in His love, deserves to receive sovereign "power"; not only is it due Him as God (by His immortal birth), but it is due Him as a conqueror through His death; and "to receive riches"—what riches? All the glory of Divinity, for, in Jesus Christ, humanity is linked to the glory of Divinity in an indivisible way! "To receive strength," "to receive honor" of everything. In a word, all is due Him . . . for Himself.

Rev. 5:13,14: And every created thing which is in heaven and on the earth and under the earth and on the sea, and all things in them, I heard saying,

"To Him who sits on the throne, and to the Lamb, be blessing and honor and glory and dominion forever and ever."
And the four living creatures kept saying, "Amen."
And the elders fell down and worshiped.

This passage shows the coming together and the harmony of all creatures who will some day give to God, with one accord, the glory due to Him.

6

Rev. 6:1,2: And I saw when the Lamb broke one of the seven seals, and I heard one of the four living creatures saying as with a voice of thunder, "Come." And I looked, and behold, a white horse, and he who sat on it had a bow; and a crown was given to him; and he went out conquering, and to conquer.

The Lamb begins to open one of the seven seals that has kept the book shut. One of the four living creatures is begging John to come and see. We, too, must go to Jesus Christ before discovering the wonder of His truth. (Do you do the opposite, by seeking truth by reasoning?) We do not find truth except as we discover Jesus Christ. Seek it in Him, and abandon yourselves to Him for that. Before the first coming of Jesus Christ, there were philosophers who tried to discover wisdom and truth; they were called wise men, but they could discover neither wisdom nor truth till Jesus Christ became incarnate. He is wisdom inborn. He revealed wisdom to men when He became man. We must then go to Jesus Christ to have truth; seeking it elsewhere is seeking error and lie. These living creatures invite us to come to Jesus Christ to discover truth in Him.

The Lamb opens one of the seven seals. "A white horse" is shown "and he that sat on the horse has a bow." This is the first state of the soul led by Jesus Christ. This is also the first age of the Church. This is a state of fighting and victory, and the more we fight, the more we conquer. Victory is crowned, and unceasingly we go from victory to victory. In our first stage all fightings are rewarded and crowned. Note then: The first living creature was the lion. The first horse is a victorious warrior.

The first state is a victory rather than a fight; the soul feels everything is easy; his enemies fall as he draws near. He is given a bow to fight from a distance; he aims with ease and wounds without receiving any wound. The beginning is a period full of sweetness; fighting enemies that are far off and whom God stops in their attacks.

> **Rev. 6:3,4: And when He broke the second seal, I heard the second living creature saying, "Come." And another, a red horse, went out; and to him who sat on it, it was granted to take peace from the earth, and that men should slay one another; and a great sword was given to him.**

In the second, things are different. The horse has not the whiteness of the first. It is red. In the first fight, faults seem to have all been washed; but in this, the soul begins to become dark.

"... and to him who sat on it, it was granted to take peace...." This is the first trial of the soul. He suffers much and now loses that sweet peace which made the presence of God so wonderful. The soul does not seem to triumph or to fight; he only feels wounded.

There is given to him a sword and he wants to use it, but only in self-defense. He only feels the wounds he receives. He attacks but is fought back. The wounds he receives hurt more than the harm he does to the enemy. Peace is lost within, and without. Why does God want "to take peace from the earth?" He wants the soul to lose the peace he had in himself, so that he will leave self. Remember, the second living creature is a calf, or bull. The fight is more violent.

> **Rev. 6:5,6: And when He broke the third seal, I heard the third living creature saying, "Come." And I looked, and behold, a black horse; and he who sat on it had a pair of scales in his hand. And I heard as it were a voice in the center of the four living creatures saying, "A quart of wheat for a**

**denarius, and three quarts of barley for a denarius;
and do not harm the oil and the wine."**

The third horse is black.

The state of the believer becomes more terrible still.
Please note, the soul is not dark, but black. "I am black but
comely," says the Song of Solomon. The fight has stopped.
The believer does not fight any more nor is he fought by his
enemies. He has balances in his hand for he is being
weighed. Everything has lost its value; what once he prized,
he now dislikes. But he does not notice that as the scale
goes down on one side, it goes up on the other, so that the
weight which brings part of himself down very low, raises
his soul to God.

The soul itself is deprived of God, and in a state of famine. This child of God had no desire for Him and, it seems,
has never been further from Him. There is a deep empti-
ness. The comforts given him are rare and costly. However,
it is forbidden "to hurt the oil and the wine." The soul is still
sustained and strengthened with a secret anointing and a
strong wine . . . although the believer is not aware of this
inner sustaining.

**Rev. 6:7,8: And when He broke the fourth seal, I
heard the voice of the fourth living creature saying, "Come." And I looked, and behold, an ashen
horse; and he who sat on it had the name Death;
and Hades was following with him. And authority
was given to them over a fourth of the earth, to kill
with sword and with famine and with pestilence
and by the wild beasts of the earth.**

The fourth living creature, the eagle, calls for death. It
seems to me that there is a contrast here between this bird
living near the sun, discovering the truth more than any,
and the fact that it calls out to see death. How is that?
Because by death only can truth and life be received. Death
was riding "an ashen horse," symbol of frightful terrors.
"Hades followed". . . it seems that in this state, the soul is
going to a sure death rushing to hell. However this death
has "power" to attack only "a fourth part of earth," which
means the last and main part, that is the senses.

What are the inventions of death to destroy? They are

four. The first is the sword, with its prickings and most sensitive pains. Then comes famine; the suffering is less painful but deeper and more cruel. Next "the beasts of the earth" come to devour and swallow this poor soul. Next all these evils unite to cause death. Such states of the soul are not imaginary. They are quite real.

> **Rev. 6:9: And when He broke the fifth seal, I saw underneath the altar the souls of those who had been slain because of the word of God, and because of the testimony which they had maintained; ...**

How beautiful is this passage! How expressive! When the soul is destroyed by a complete, continual and total sacrifice, "the souls of those who had been slain because of the word of God" appear under the altar! This is not only true of the martyrs who are martyrs in their body but more truly of the martyrs who suffer for the inward life. These are sometimes killed in body. Others are "killed" by writings, slanders and persecutions. After all, it is an inner Spirit, an internal witness that we sense inside, and which we announce, that is the first cause of all persecutions.

> **Rev. 6:10: ... and they cried out with a loud voice, saying, "How long, O Lord, holy and true, wilt Thou refrain from judging and avenging our blood on those who dwell on the earth?"**

Have you noted that the fact that persecution is going on at any given time is — for the longest time — hidden from common knowledge? The Lord uses this time of unseen, unheralded persecution against His servants to bring them to nought. It seems that God is for a while on the oppressor's side; but a time comes when these souls being set free from every bondage ask to be avenged; the Spirit is doing it for them.

> **Rev. 6:11: And there was given to each of them a white robe, and they were told that they should rest for a little while longer, until the number of their fellow servants and their brethren who were to be killed even as they had been, should be completed also.**

After God's servants have gone through the states mentioned above, a new life is given them, "the white robes" of innocence. They are delivered of every evil ... but they are not avenged. There comes for them, rest.

Rev. 6:12,13: And I looked when He broke the sixth seal, and there was a great earthquake; and the sun became black as sackcloth made of hair, and the whole moon became like blood; and the stars of the sky fell to the earth, as a fig tree casts its unripe figs when shaken by a great wind.

This passage shows several things happening at the same time.

First, part of what will take place at the end of times is described. Secondly, God's vengeance on those who are the persecutors of saints is revealed. Thirdly, a description is given of certain states which believers pass through.

It is certain that God will bring into strange terrors those who persecute His servants. They will see the evil they did; they will be shown the truth about their crimes. "The sun" of their understanding will be darkened; "the moon," represents their memory. Abel's blood will come to their mind; for Abel was, from the beginning of this world, the picture of inward souls that have been stripped and who love purely. For Abel offered a pure sacrifice. Today the same things are occurring and Abel's blood cries out without ceasing.

"The stars fall to earth," means that the light man has falls and fails.

Concerning the meaning of this passage as being applied to the souls in whom God works with extreme hardness in His mercy and justice, "the sun" of righteousness hides, becomes dark; "the moon" becomes blood. They only have thoughts of death; graces usually extended to these believers seem to have fallen to the ground.

Rev. 6:14–17: And the sky was split apart like a scroll when it is rolled up; and every mountain and island were moved out of their places. And the kings of the earth and the great men and the commanders and the rich and the strong and every slave and free man, hid themselves in the caves

and among the rocks of the mountains; and they said to the mountains and to the rocks, "Fall on us and hide us from the presence of Him who sits on the throne, and from the wrath of the Lamb; for the great day of their wrath has come; and who is able to stand?"

For those who persecuted the saints, "heaven will depart"; that is every help from above and every hope on earth will be taken from them. It seems God will never be merciful; they ask the mountains to hide them, seeking a place of refuge, but they find it too late, through grief and strange turmoil.

Let us look at this passage from the view of the believer, one who feels estranged from God's mercy. Here too, heaven is rolled up as a scroll – they no longer have access into heaven; all hope is withdrawn; but, when Heaven opens up, they will find it more favorable than it had seemed hard. Until then they may be utterly desolate. They think they will find "some mountain" to flee to (some consolation in strong and spiritual persons who are like "mountains" through the eminence of their graces, or on those who are like "rocks" by their steadfastness). This is a state for souls strong in God. This was the state for Jesus Christ in the garden of Gethsemane when He bore the sins of mankind. This terrible weight made Him sweat drops of blood, and this wrath lasted till He died. Oh, who will be able to survive in such a state? God must clothe the soul with a superhuman strength. The soul must bear these inner states that Jesus Christ bore, but he must have Jesus Christ in these states.

7

Rev. 7:1-3: After this I saw four angels standing at the four corners of the earth, holding back the four winds of the earth, so that no wind should blow on the earth or on the sea or on any tree. And I saw another angel ascending from the rising of the sun, having the seal of the living God; and he cried out with a loud voice to the four angels to whom it was granted to harm the earth and the sea, saying, "Do not harm the earth or the sea or the trees, until we have sealed the bond-servants of our God on their foreheads."

When God wants to punish those who persecute His servants (or when He wishes to work His Life into those who are entirely devoted to Him), He stops all the sweet and comforting influences . . . whether they come from within or without. Every refreshing is removed. Before God pours His wrath on persecutors – and so that the saints may not be involved in that punishment – the Lord prevents the devil from having any power over these believers; therefore God marks them with His seal. God takes these souls under His protection and all the plagues of the devil and sin do not come near any longer. These will not be hurt in the general punishment which God will send on earth, nor will they be hurt in the final judgment.

Rev. 7:4: And I heard the number of those who were sealed, one hundred and forty-four thousand sealed from every tribe of the sons of Israel: . . .

The mark of this seal (the sign for all the inner souls) is for those marked with the characteristics of the Spirit of God. See how the number of these saints grow, and how they come from all lands, as the end approaches.

Oh, our Lord, only in eternity will we know the number of the inner souls You have stamped with Your seal.

These are the true children of Israel who will not be overwhelmed in the total ruin of Egypt.

Rev. 7:9,10: After these things I looked, and behold, a great multitude, which no one could count, from every nation and all tribes and peoples and tongues, standing before the throne and before the Lamb, clothed in white robes, and palm branches were in their hands; and they cry out with a loud voice saying, "Salvation to our God, who sits on the throne, and to the Lamb."

Besides the saints marked with the particular characteristics of the inner life, there are countless more saints. Oh God, there is no place, land or nation where You do not show Your mercy. Only in eternity will we see the greatness and extent of Your mercies.

All these saints are standing, which shows their steadfastness, their confidence. They are dressed in white dresses because they have been renewed with the robe of innocence. Seals that have been opened until now are the truth that has been manifested. What is this truth which was so sealed, so unknown? That full salvation of our whole being belongs to God alone. He alone must work that completed salvation in each soul. We do not see in us any merit for such a great blessing. It is His doing. The Saints in heaven will never be able to see salvation in themselves or anything that made their salvation sure. They will endlessly sing that salvation belongs to God. This will be our joy.

Rev. 7:11,12: And all the angels were standing around the throne and around the elders and the four living creatures; and they fell on their faces before the throne and worshiped God, saying, "Amen, blessing and glory and wisdom and thanksgiving and honor and power and might, be to our God forever and ever. Amen."

Men have an advantage over angels; they can suffer for God. But elect angels have an advantage over men: They do not sin. This advantage comes from their constant nothingness, and the fact that they come not out from this nothingness. If man reaches this state of being in a continuous nothingness, he shares the happiness of the angel. When John said, "they fell on their faces," he meant they remain in a continuous nothingness, "before the throne" of God. Few men, and that by grace, share the angels' happiness. Such ones are on their faces because they are nothing.

Some angels once stepped out of their state of nothingness, rising against God; this made them sin and brought them in hell. The angel Lucifer came out of his nothingness without any means of entering again. Man, on the contrary, may re-enter this state, by the grace of God's salvation. Saul is like Lucifer. He sinned and remained in his rebellion. David sinned, but humbled himself and entered again into his relationship with God.

"Verily every man at his best state is altogether vanity" (Ps. 39:5). Nothingness is all that is left for us, therefore. A man in nothingness does not oppose God's will. If there is opposition in you to God's will you are not dead and you come out of nothingness.

Jesus Christ Who is the model for all prayers fell on His face to worship, not so much to teach us an outward posture as to show us the attitude in which our soul must be as we pray and worship. In this inward state of nothingness the soul gives God all the glory that can be given to the Creator by one of His creatures.

Therefore, the angels say that blessing, glory, wisdom, thanksgiving, honor, power and might belong to our God here! Their state of nothingness accomplishes all these acts of gratefulness and homage to the sovereignty of God; only this state can do this with absolute purity. He who is nothing, before Him, acknowledges Him as the only Sovereign Being. The believer ceases to be all that he is so that God alone will be. With all the words of honor and gratefulness we use to God, we honor Him as a creature and not as God, since we do towards Him what we do in behalf of our sovereigns and benefactors; therefore honoring Him through nothingness, we honor Him as God.

How did Jesus Christ teach us to honor God as God? He became nothing, taking the form of a servant. In this way, He gave God such a high honor, though being God Himself, that a greater honor cannot be found. In this nothingness of His, He accomplishes His wonderful works! So, too, we do His will as it is done in heaven, for that is what nothingness always does.

Remember, God created all things with nothing. By using nothingness He does His greatest things. Till man has reached this state of nothingness, God may hardly have a way to use him because the man is always stealing His glory.

> **Rev. 7:13,14: And one of the elders answered, saying to me, "These who are clothed in the white robes, who are they, and from where have they come?" And I said to him, "My lord, you know." And he said to me, "These are the ones who come out of the great tribulation, and they have washed their robes and made them white in the blood of the Lamb."**

The soul is no sooner brought to nought than he is clothed with the robe of innocence. When God sends His Spirit, bringing this soul to nought, he is created anew. A new creature in Jesus Christ! He clothes him with Jesus Christ. These men, then, dressed in white, are lowly, unassuming, and emptied souls.

But where did they come from? From out of themselves! They have passed through total destruction! Their robes were stained by sin, covered by the dust ... but through the loss of themselves, "their robes were washed in the blood of the Lamb."

Oh, blood of the divine, spotless Lamb, You are a purifier bringing the soul into an admirable purity. Those who find no strength, purity, holiness in themselves are obliged to come out from themselves and plunge into the blood of the Lamb, whence they come out in an unheard of purity through a complete abandonment.

Oh men who believe you can by your cares whiten your robes, you are mistaken; you will become more dirty! You only soil what you hold. But, if you want to whiten them, throw them into purity itself! There they lose their stain and are given a divine purity.

Rev. 7:15,16: "For this reason, they are before the throne of God; and they serve Him day and night in His temple; and He who sits on the throne shall spread His tabernacle over them. They shall hunger no more, neither thirst anymore; neither shall the sun beat down on them, nor any heat; . . ."

The Christian, now totally emptied, is in an intimate and permanent union. His internal spirit is always "before the throne of God," constantly before Him and with Him, and one with His throne. God wants no creature to be perfectly independent. He wants that one pliable and doing His every will. This is the state of a believer in nothingness, no longer with a will of his own; he (always doing the will of God) thus serves Him night and day, inwardly, being the temple of God. The work of this one is the continual union of Will to will. That is the greatest service that men can render Him. This is the very service Jesus Christ rendered on earth to His Father.

See now the reward of their work! What happens to them? He Who sits on His throne makes their heart His throne. He dwells there, abiding permanently in them as He had promised in His Gospel.

"If anyone does the will of My Father, We will come to him, We will take our abode with him."

"They shall hunger no more, neither thirst any more." Why? They are fully satisfied. (They have no will of their own, they have no desire, no inclination. They are not molested by the heat of sin; they are refreshed and joyful. No one can understand this state except the one who experiences it.) The believing one who has come thus far is free, because truth and nothingness are the same thing. Truth is the expression, while nothingness is the operation.

Rev. 7:17: ". . . for the Lamb in the center of the throne shall be their shepherd, and shall guide them to springs of the water of life; and God shall wipe every tear from their eyes."

This divine Shepherd does not wish any other staff to lead them than that of the cross. Then, after leading them with this cross in the frightful and terrible places of the desert where they see only dark places, where there is no water to quench their thirst, He leads them into the bosom of God, and God is their fountain of living water. There they are refreshed by Himself.

If the Father is the spring, Jesus is the river of delight running from that Spring. They are refreshed forever, and they thirst no more. God wipes away their tears.

8

Rev. 8:1–4: And when He broke the seventh seal, there was silence in heaven for about half an hour. And I saw the seven angels who stand before God; and seven trumpets were given to them. And another angel came and stood at the altar, holding a golden censer; and much incense was given to him, that he might add it to the prayers of all the saints upon the golden altar which was before the throne. And the smoke of the incense, with the prayers of the saints, went up before God out of the angel's hand.

Who would think, after the believing one has reached the state of nothingness, that there should be another seal to be opened? It seems all is done. It is true that on the believer's side, all is done, but there remains a seal which will manifest this truth to others.

Before this takes place, the inward parts of this one are placed in a state of silence.

After "the seven trumpets given to the seven angels standing before God" are announced, then prayer and intercession for others are given to these. These prayers are enclosed in a pure will . . . as in a "golden censer." There, with the "fire" of love, the prayers are melted together before God. These prayers are continual sacrifices going up before God.

This is the state of the bride of whom it was said: "Who is this that cometh out of the wilderness like pillars of smoke, perfumed with myrrh and frankincense?" These prayers, prayed in different places by different persons, are gathered and offered to God on His altar because they are according to His will.

This kind of prayer is pure, and it is simple.

Rev. 8:5: And the angel took the censer; and he filled it with the fire of the altar and threw it to the earth; and there followed peals of thunder and sounds and flashes of lightning and an earthquake.

When God wants to pour His pure love on the earth, He commissions the angel to take "the censer" (which is the will and heart of that praying one) and He fills the censer with the "fire" of love. Where does He take this fire? From the altar of the Will of God.

What happens when these blessed seven Spirits cast on the earth this fire which produces such lovely blazes? There are "thunderings." There arise persecutions, strange murmurs against these believers, in which the inner grace is outpoured. Did You not say that You came to throw a fire on the earth and that You wanted it to be kindled?

Nothing can quench this divine fire.

Pour it forth upon the earth again, oh Lord!

Rev. 8:6: And the seven angels who had the seven trumpets prepared themselves to sound them.

When God sends His fire on earth, He stirs apostolic men to announce His truth, and through this fire to bring destruction, destruction even as far as the self life of man.

Rev. 8:7: And the first sounded, and there came hail and fire, mixed with blood, and they were thrown to the earth; and a third of the earth was burned up, and a third of the trees were burned up, and all the green grass was burned up.

When the spirit of sacrifice increases on earth and truth begins to be announced there will be "hail" – or tempests – to prevent it. Those who persecute the spirit of sacrifice will rain fire.

The same thing happens to us individually. "Hail" falls on His holy ones, a hail of outward (and often inward) sufferings. This fire is "mixed with blood," which means it is not pure. But though this fire is not purified, it consumes the strength of self.

Rev. 8:8,9: And the second angel sounded, and something like a great mountain burning with fire was thrown into the sea; and a third of the sea became blood; and a third of the creatures, which were in the sea and had life, died; and a third of the ships were destroyed.

The fire now changes the sea into blood. The soul loses its ability to feel, taste, see, hear and touch. All is taken, and this causes the second death!

We must know that "Revelation" is not only a revelation of the last judgments, but it is a prophecy of what must happen to the Church of God, especially in the end when it will spread throughout all the earth. This book is written outside and inside because it is the inward and outward truth of Jesus Christ—and His Church which will be manifested everywhere. Since this inward and outward truth must be discovered to all men, the signs thus described must be taken—not literally—but with the meaning the Holy Spirit gives.

"A mountain" of anger, of fury, of "fire." A mountain of intense spiritual fire will be cast into the Church. Men powerful in words will arise and change the third part of this sea into blood, tears, afflictions and "the third part of the creatures in the sea died."

Those that are dead will not be changed.

Oh God, You will do it for Your glory, and this will be unveiled to those who will be given light.

Rev. 8:10,11: And the third angel sounded, and a great star fell from heaven, burning like a torch, and it fell on a third of the rivers and on the springs of waters; and the name of the star is called Wormwood; and a third of the waters became wormwood; and many men died from the waters, because they were made bitter.

The third herald of the truth has no sooner finished sounding the trumpet than "there fell a great star from heaven." This star, that which has guided the soul, falls in such a way that "the rivers" of grace and comfort are changed into "bitterness" and grief. Only "the third part is bitter," though it seems to the soul that all has been changed into bitterness. The divine delights of these rivers were flowing when this star shone in his understanding; all this is changed into "wormwood." It seems he will have no pleasure ever in life. This state causes the "death" of reasoning and understanding.

The "self-mind" will never die except by the fall of this large star.

> **Rev. 8:12,13: And the fourth angel sounded, and a third of the sun and a third of the moon and a third of the stars were smitten, so that a third of them might be darkened and the day might not shine for a third of it, and the night in the same way. And I looked, and I heard an eagle flying in mid-heaven, saying with a loud voice, "Woe, woe, woe, to those who dwell on the earth, because of the remaining blasts of the trumpet of the three angels who are about to sound!"**

Oh God, what grief and desolation is brought to the earth by this fourth angel, for You enlighten only by bringing darkness. Every self light must be destroyed to enter into the light of truth. These things happen, to the Church and to the individual, so they might be placed in reality. In this great disaster the lights of the Church and the holy ones will not be totally put out and the darkness will not be forever.

What message do we see here for ourselves? That if the third part of the soul will be in darkness, it still retains much light which does not show. The believer, suffering darkness, must taste the deepest woes before enjoying the highest benefits.

9

Rev. 9:1,2: And the fifth angel sounded, and I saw a star from heaven which had fallen to the earth; and the key of the bottomless pit was given to him. And he opened the bottomless pit; and smoke went up out of the pit, like the smoke of a great furnace; and the sun and the air were darkened by the smoke of the pit.

The fifth angel sounds. A star falls.

When you see a "star" fall, it is one who once had the truth who has fallen. He has the key to the pit. He is one with the other fallen stars. The devil is permitted to side with them and they create a horrible "smoke" of murmurs and backbiting, and truth even is darkened. "The air" is affected by this; everybody gives credit to the fallen star and his lies; the princes of the Church, the sun, are darkened by a crowd of these false accusers rising against these persons. Oh hellish pit, you vomit your last fire, my Master allowing this until all woes have come that are necessary.

But we see still another meaning to this scene of a falling star.

This woe, outwardly horrible, is the start of great happiness. The star falls; no light remains, and "the key of the bottomless pit" is given to him. A vile stench and wicked smokes are the only things that appear, the most unfortunate temptations. Here is "a great furnace" of human miseries. All these things do befall the one, in any age, who is seeking rest . . . and the fullness of God's truth.

Rev. 9:3,4: And out of the smoke came forth locusts upon the earth; and power was given them, as the scorpions of the earth have power. And they were told that they should not hurt the grass of the earth, nor any green thing, nor any tree, but only the men who do not have the seal of God on their foreheads.

Watching God in this unfolding drama, we would think that destruction is all He has in mind. He seems to be quenching truth instead of establishing it. These are your Master's strokes, and – as God – He acts mostly this way.

Oh men, how blind you are in thinking you can fathom God's dealings in souls, and in believing that – if you do not understand something – it therefore cannot be of God! You deal with God worse than you do with the most ignorant men. You will at least acknowledge that there are men on this earth who know about things of which you are ignorant. But you will not give this same ground to God.

He forbids the "locusts" "to hurt," but He allows "the men which have not the seal of God" to be hurt. We ought to know that in man are two lives: One is carnal; the other bears the characteristics of God, and is sealed. The soul that is sealed by God is pure and whole in Him. But the corrupt, carnal man, the sinner, will not be spared. But if they hurt God's servants' bodies or souls, their spirit will be freer than ever when overwhelmed with plagues.

Rev. 9:5,6: And they were not permitted to kill anyone, but to torment for five months; and their torment was like the torment of a scorpion when it stings a man. And in those days men will seek death and will not find it; and they will long to die and death flees from them.

"In those days" of desolation and trial, "shall men seek death and shall not find it." Oh God, what a comfort for such a person to die! But the soul fears to displease God more than it fears a thousand deaths. It does not want to die to end its misery but only to avoid sin. Oh, men who go through this state, suffer! And you will see that truth united with wisdom will bring all desired comforts. "Death" seems "to flee" instead of coming near because the soul is not afraid of death. However sin, which seems real, causes all grief, and death is counted to be a great gain. The more the soul asks for deliverance, the more the evil increases until that soul knows how to yield to God the rest of her life.

Let us look at this passage, now, from another view. Can this passage also refer to the average servants of God in the Church? They are stung and wounded by poisoned tongues which create cruel crosses. Power was given to the locust to torment them five months, but will not be able "to kill" them, neither by the death to sin which will lead them to impatience, nor by natural death. Nevertheless, God will save many of His servants. He will permit them to be afflicted, to the limit . . . but not killed. Paul said, of himself (II Cor. 6:9): "We are chastened but not killed". The Lord says that all this is true, and must happen this way in the Church of God, and in the lives of the servants of God.

Rev. 9:7–11: And the appearance of the locusts was like horses prepared for battle; and on their heads, as it were, crowns like gold, and their faces were like the faces of men. And they had hair like the hair of women, and their teeth were like the teeth of lions. And they had breastplates like breastplates of iron; and the sound of their wings was like the sound of chariots, of many horses rushing to battle. And they have tails like scorpions, and stings; and in their tails is their power to hurt men for five months. They have as king over them, the angel of the abyss; his name in Hebrew is Abaddon, and in the Greek he has the name Apollyon.

God takes pleasure in the description of these locusts, so wondrous. Whether we look at this scene as the world as a whole at the end time, or whether we view it as a thing which happens to individual believers and God's designs in their lives . . . regardless, there is nothing here to frighten us. These who are to torment God's servants are "like horses prepared for battle," for it is certain that they are fighting the most terrible war that will ever be. There is no stronger war than that which is going on between the forces of darkness and the interior one.

Such have been their ways through the centuries.

"Their hair," "as the hair of women," signifying that these persons have an artificial sweetness, catching the innocent in their net, and winning the "lookers on" to their strange viewpoint. But they have teeth of lions, teeth not seen until it is too late, and with which they heartlessly tear the innocent.

We see "breastplates of iron"; they cover themselves with pretexts which make them unconquerable. They attack, wound, knock down without fear of being hurt. "The sound of their wings" – their fame, flying everywhere, winning for them many people – is "as the sound of chariots, of many horses running to battle"; it seems to everyone that these people are equipped with zeal to defend the cause of God, proclaiming loudly their success, the defeat of others, the advantage of siding with their interests which are (they say) God's. They point to their success as proof. But if their face seems human, "their tails," which are not seen so long as they only show their face, are like scorpions'. How dangerous! What damage! Yet God gave them their power in order to sanctify His servants.

But though these beings have power from God, he who stirs them and makes them act is the angel of the bottomless pit. He wants to make an end of the servants of God, perceiving that God wants to use them to extend His kingdom and destroy Satan's kingdom. He does his best to remove them from the face of the earth. But instead of doing away with them, he removes, in them, what is opposed to God.

Rev. 9:12: The first woe is past; behold, two woes are still coming after these things.

Who would not believe this is the end at the sight of these evils? How happy we would be if they ended there! You are indeed mercilessly cruel, oh God. Your cruelty appears; but the more it appears, the more it hides an infinite mercy. What seems sweet holds a tail full of poison, but what seems most cruel is full of sweetness.

Rev. 9:13-15: And the sixth angel sounded, and I heard a voice from the four horns of the golden

altar which is before God, one saying to the sixth angel who had the trumpet, "Release the four angels who are bound at the great river Euphrates." And the four angels, who had been prepared for the hour and day and month and year, were released, so that they might kill a third of mankind.

The sixth herald is that of death. All that has happened till now has been prepared for death, but death has not arrived. Without this death, truth will never be manifested to men. The voice giving the command comes out of the golden altar where the last sacrifice must be made, the most terrible and strange of all sacrifices.

Oh righteousness of God, how cruel you are! You want only death. But how sweet and kind You are to this one who has no other interest than God's only, who has no more self interest, who being placed in this reality as an experience — worships, blesses and loves this apparent cruelty, given for so great a benefit. Your approach is rough and cruel, but Your cruelty afterward changes into floods of delight. Oh, mystery of cruelty! Mystery of love and sweetness! Who will understand these? He whom Thou hast spared least is often the happiest. Oh Righteousness, we fear You because we do not know You. You are cruel only to those who oppose the Kingdom of pure love; but You are kind and gracious to the one who, having no more self-love, cannot oppose pure love. How far from the purity of love is the one who still fears Thee! Oh Righteousness, whoever does not love You with the most extreme passion is not yet free from himself, though he may think he is. You are only in the hearts for which divine righteousness, in its most extreme severity, has only charms and sweetnesses.

There are believers for whom love has sweetnesses; they think they are well dealt with; there are others who have only hardships and they think they are to be pitied. The greatest sweetness of love is receiving none!

All the afflictions that have come up to this time could not cause death because "these angels were bound." Up to now, abandonment has always survived with vigor and strength; that is, all the soul gained through suffering was its surrender without reserve. The soul wanted death and became resigned to die or not to die. The soul resigned to die when she feared death; then it resigned not to die when death was welcomed. She thinks she is delivered. The soul is surprised to see that all this served to prepare it for another fight which is so much harder because it has tasted the sweetness of rest and quiet.

It is a very surprising thing for a believer to realize that the duration of suffering makes suffering bearable. One gets used to it. But God, to harden us, causes suffering to cease when we get used to it! He gives much rest so that the return to suffering will be all the more effective. The first loss of abandonment is imperfect. It contains spite, anger, and rebellion, till the soul realizes it makes them worse by resisting them. As the believer yields, they diminish and end; abandonment becomes then stronger and broader. When abandonment is without measure, the soul may even be delivered of its pains.

There is however a greater abandonment!

This greater abandonment is like a river which carries you without mercy, but which also leads you! This river is as a ship going into the deep from which you dive to drown and die. Without this abandonment, we never leave self; we always remain proprietors. Without the loss of conscious abandonment, we never get perfectly lost in God. We sail on this immense Ocean with abandonment but we are not fully lost in God unless we lose this abandonment of which we are conscious.

Fortunately, the loss of this abandonment does not cause the griefs and anger of old. The Lord must give a special power to lose sight of our abandonment. But how? And when?

"In the day, hour, month and year" which God has appointed for this. My God, how beautiful these words are and what great things they contain! They show us the most wonderful providence that ever was. A soul that is led unreservedly by its God will find this wonderful providence, causing that soul to do everything at the right time, according to God's will and the desire of the soul. All dangers in the spiritual life come because we want to grow without the help of God. All must be done by God, in His appointed time; He knows the state in which we are and reveals this to the soul. We must then patiently wait for the hour, the time, the moment.

Thus the soul loses its conscious abandonment and enters into true death.

> **Rev. 9:16–19: And the number of the armies of the horsemen was two hundred million; I heard the number of them. And this is how I saw in the vision of the horses and those who sat on them: the riders had breastplates the color of fire and of hyacinth and of brimstone; and the heads of the horses are like the heads of lions; and out of their mouths proceed fire and smoke and brimstone. A third of mankind was killed by these three plagues, by the fire and the smoke and the brimstone, which proceeded out of their mouths. For the power of the horses is in their mouths and in their tails; for their tails are like serpents and have heads; and with them they do no harm.**

The evils which come to overwhelm these souls are multiplied endlessly. An army comes which grows bigger every day. The troubles surround, increase and multiply like the sand of the sea, outside and inside; each day sees the birth of a new one. People who are contrary to them increase and multiply. Nature, hell, and men are set against the souls that are abandoned to God. Those who arrived for the fight have "breastplates the color of fire" because they are dressed with anger, fire which they pretend is godly zeal. These breastplates have the color of "hyacinth" because they wrap themselves with righteousness. The devil is "the horse" they mount, and he has "the heads of lions." He is full of strength and fury, stirring people to destroy the men who serve God. This fire and brimstone are a strong persecution which can come from hell only; the smoke is the noise of persecution. "Their tails are like serpents"; because they use, with skill, crafty devices to hide the blows they give.

The soul is surrounded by all evils, deprived of all benefits. The fury of hell seems uncontrolled. Oh God, where can we go? There is no place to flee to.

Oh, happy are those who then are without help and stay! They truly die. Those who are sustained and helped lose much. Oh, if we knew the wrong done to the soul which is not completely left in the hand of God! Instead of saving it, we lose it.

Rev. 9:20–21: And the rest of mankind, who were not killed by these plagues, did not repent of the works of their hands, so as not to worship demons, and the idols of gold and of silver and of brass.

Certainly all these things will in time come to pass. Here two things are referred to; one is the conversion of sinners, the call to the godless to faith; the other is the destruction of _____. [An untranslatable word follows here, the French word "propriete." This word – ownership of self – is used often by Madame Guyon. It has a broad meaning referring to a desire to possess things.] To stop this call the devil strengthens the idolaters, hardens the sinners and creates a fight against spirituality (godliness). As he opposes righteousness, evil increases and the godly are fought and destroyed. More strength is acquired by the wicked till the set time when God will put an end to the troubles given to the saints, and to the crimes of their adversaries.

Men who do not come into truth through their sufferings do not repent of their doings and of the works of their hands. These are not troubled. They will see frightful wars, strange sufferings, and horrible famines; yet most of them will be hardened. Those held by "ownership of self" are strengthened in their carnal ways through the persecution of the saints.

(It is certain you must die to self to lose the sense of carnality and enter into truth, otherwise you remain more attached to your own works; you take credit for things which belong only to God. You build everything on your works; you become an idolater because you love yourself. You prefer yourself to the interests of God; you prefer a lie to the truth. This is the worship of demons.)

Some hold on to money, others to honor, others to themselves, others to an imagined and unreal virtue and to idols which can neither hear nor instruct nor lead them.

We see that the world will not repent. Oh God, what corruption! Have mercy on Your Church! Voices are raised against those who worship God in their heart; they are fought against, persecuted and not one voice is raised against those who have in their heart impurity, envy, adultery, hatred.

Are some even canonized? Esteemed? Applauded? And those disgraced and considered as the worst of men are, on the contrary, burning with pure love, shun glory, honor, esteem of men, looking only to God – their only aim!

Evil is become good, and good, . . . evil!

10

Rev. 10:1,2: And I saw another strong angel coming down out of heaven, clothed with a cloud; and the rainbow was upon his head, and his face was like the sun, and his feet like pillars of fire; and he had in his hand a little book which was open. And he placed his right foot on the sea and his left on the land; . . .

Though sufferings may appear cruel and strange, they are the cause of all benefits. When they drive us to despair, we are near the greatest wealth. The last woes seemed without remedy; the servants of God and followers of truth seemed destroyed by those who help lies to triumph and reign. Sin has become stronger and virtue is gone from the earth; God even seems to aid in causing this situation, driving away the virtuous ones. (There is some truth in this, since He wants to destroy in them any carnality that did not come from Him.)

Oh death, oh misfortunes, oh losses, oh despairs, what good comes from you! You bring life, joy, possession and salvation!

An angel, so strong and mighty, comes after the destruction! Nothing is stronger; all other forces compared with this one are very weak. Here we see truth, divine truth; this truth came down and the Book of truth comes to earth to be discovered.

Oh truth, ignored, buried, bound, hidden till now, you are going to be made known! This angel is "clothed with a cloud," to let us know that however clear truth may be in this life, it is always accompanied by some cloud. It is not so in heaven. This angel had "a rainbow upon his head," a sign of general reconciliation and of changelessness, and steady and perfect peace on the part of God for men. Error and lie have drawn God's anger on earth; truth is going to bring peace, quietness and joy. Oh peace, so fought and spoken against, you will be victorious!

"The face" of the herald is like "the Sun" because truth dispels the darkness of error and of lying, as the day dispels the night. All darkness and night comes from the absence of the sun, as the day exists by its presence; even so all errors, wanderings, and ignorance come from the absence of Truth, as all lights by its presence.

"His feet" are "as pillars of fire," to show that truth is founded on a firm and unchangeable love.

The book he had in his hand points to the manifestation of this truth and on the land shows that this *truth* must be shown everywhere, even inwardly and outwardly.

Rev. 10:3,4: . . . and he cried out with a loud voice, as when a lion roars; and when he had cried out, the seven peals of thunder uttered their voices. And when the seven peals of thunder had spoken, I was about to write; and I heard a voice from heaven saying, "Seal up the things which the seven peals of thunder have spoken, and do not write them."

The Truth will be announced with such might by the voice of the "Lion" who has been chosen to manifest that Truth to the world, that there is no corner in the earth where it will not be heard. But while this Herald of truth announces truth to the whole earth, there are "seven thunders" of the truth. But though the noise of these thunders is heard everywhere, what their voices express is known only by John, and the few persons it pleases God to show.

There are two things in truth, one that must be published to everybody, the other that must be sealed and hidden, because the world cannot take it. He to whom it is shown must keep it within.

Oh truth, hidden in the midst of sufferings, who could understand you? If you were uncovered and announced, who could hear? You are enclosed in the depth of the heart of those to whom you revealed yourself.

There are seven voices of the truth that must not be uncovered to men. They are hidden because of the corruption of men.

> **Rev. 10:5-7: And the angel whom I saw standing on the sea and on the land lifted up his right hand to heaven, and swore by Him who lives forever and ever, who created heaven and the things in it, and the earth and the things in it, and the sea and the things in it, that there shall be delay no longer, but in the days of the voice of the seventh angel, when he is about to sound, then the mystery of God is finished, as He preached to His servants the prophets.**

The angel swore that time would be no longer. But for manifesting hidden truth, the last herald of truth must sound the trumpet, or it will not appear.

I shall be known, says this Truth, but I shall not be listened to and understood. Afterward, I will be heard and understood and I will give the understanding of my mystery, when the time will be ripe; but the time for my being heard is far and the time for my being understood is still farther.

> **Rev. 10:8: And the voice which I heard from heaven, I heard again speaking with me, and saying, "Go, take the book which is open in the hand of the angel who stands on the sea and on the land."**

This last voice, that of the sixth angel, came from the altar of sacrifices. It is also the voice that performs the last sacrifice. It comes from God Himself. Oh Voice, how frightful, sweet and charming you are! This same voice orders John to take the little book from the hand of the angel. It is a command, a mission to publish the truth.

Oh God, You have had, You do have, heralds of the truth, but what persecution they have met, and will meet!

> **Rev. 10:9: And I went to the angel, telling him to give me the little book. And he said to me, "Take**

it, and eat it; and it will make your stomach bitter, but in your mouth it will be sweet as honey."

Truth must be devoured; the soul must receive it, eat it, devour it; then the soul will be devoured by the truth. It must be received in the soul before it is given to others!

All that is not given out by experience is not a true light.

We must be placed in truth before teaching it. We must, like John, not only have heard the truth but we must have understood and experienced it ... before showing it to others!

But no sooner is it received and devoured than the stomach is bitter and the mouth, sweet. Truth has something so sweet for the will, typified by the mouth, that it is a delight to the soul. What joy and satisfaction for the soul to which truth is communicated! But in the belly is bitterness; and this is the difference between the truth which is manifested to the soul for its own benefit and truth which is given to the soul for others. As long as truth is given only for the Christian's own benefit, it is only sweetness. But when it is given for others, all the inner parts are full of pain. What pains, weariness, slanders!

Paul assured us that he bore his dear spiritual children when he saw them going astray (Gal. 4:19). I challenge anyone to be able to understand what these pains are if they do not share in such an experience.

Rev. 10:10–11: And I took the little book out of the angel's hand and ate it, and it was in my mouth sweet as honey; and when I had eaten it, my stomach was made bitter. And they said to me, "You must prophesy again concerning many peoples and nations and tongues and kings."

John admits that there was for him the greatest sweetness when he received the truth, but after devouring it he suffers untold "bitterness" inwardly. Right away he is told to prophesy before the nations. He has to show this truth in many places, before peoples and before kings. All the sufferings that the saints have before reaching the knowledge of the truth when they are saints for themselves only, are not to be compared to the sufferings endured by the apostolic men appointed to help others. God has them to go through many states, with more hardships and depth than if they were only to take care of their own sanctification. God wants to give them the light of their experience, so as not to make a mistake in directing souls. Therefore a great discernment is given them. They have borne and are acquainted with so many weaknesses that now they are not surprised at any weaknesses in others. Jesus Christ took our nature to teach us that in order to be truly compassionate, we must touch the same weaknesses others have.

11

Rev. 11:1,2: **And there was given me a measuring rod like a staff; and someone said, "Rise and measure the temple of God, and the altar, and those who worship in it. And leave out the court which is outside the temple, and do not measure it, for it has been given to the nations; and they will tread under foot the holy city for forty-two months."**

A rod was given the Apostle to measure all things justly and undisturbed. Unless this rod is given to measure all things as God sees them, we usually form judgments on souls by what they say, by what is fine, alluring, serene, adjusted; we judge them by what we feel or do not feel. To do this is to make a great mistake. Is a soul full of carnality regarded highly while the greatest of another is not because he is in extreme poverty?

The soul that is placed in the truth judges only according to truth, hence the measuring rod. The soul overlooked by leaders will be known for what it is by those persons in a similar state. The measurement is the temple of God and the altar . . . the greatness of sacrifice and worship of God, and general loss of carnality.

The outward court is not measured, because it is given unto the Gentiles. God permits much to fall on the "outer court" because He wants the believer who lives in the "outer court" to come to nought through suffering.

Rev. 11:3–5: **"And I will grant authority to my two witnesses, and they will prophesy for twelve hun-**

dred and sixty days, clothed in sackcloth." These are the two olive trees and the two lampstands that stand before the Lord of the earth. And if anyone desires to harm them, fire proceeds out of their mouth and devours their enemies; and if anyone would desire to harm them, in this manner he must be killed.

John describes here the advent of Jesus Christ — His inward and outward reign throughout the whole earth and what must take place during and before this time. Redemption through Jesus Christ has been somewhat bound and captive, and did not have its full expansion, but in the future it must be without limit or measure, and in its fullness, not only in the redeemed, as in the days past, but in all the world.

Jesus Christ came to destroy and ruin the empire of the devil throughout the whole earth. This empire has been ruined in many hearts and numberless souls to which Jesus Christ extended full redemption, but this has not become universal. The devil has kept his rights on people. But in this scene we see that he will be completely banished from the face of the earth. Jesus Christ will extend His Empire to the ends of the earth. Then all the kings of the earth will recognize Him as King. Then the wolf and the lamb will live together, and the bottomless pit will be shut.

God chooses two witnesses whom He will clothe with strength and power to announce truth. These witnesses will be clothed in sackcloths, which means they will have a plain unnoticed appearance.

These two witnesses are faith and pure love and they are under the blame of all, as a sacrifice. Faith lives only with sacrifice and pure love only in self-denial. These two witnesses declare the truth to those who are to hear their profound word.

Strong and effective words defeat all those that oppose them, forcing men to come to the truth and never more fight it. If they do not enter the truth, God will soon take them out of the world.

God bears, hides, even seems to favor the enemies, but a day will come when they will be destroyed by the words of His mouth. These servants will have no other weapon except these words of destroying fire.

We see a little of this today—holy ones who have no other weapon to defend themselves except their love and faith of which they speak and which makes their enemies speechless. God gives them words that no one can withstand.

> **Rev. 11:6: These have the power to shut up the sky, in order that rain may not fall during the days of their prophesying; and they have power over the waters to turn them into blood, and to smite the earth with every plague, as often as they desire.**

It is certain that those to whom power is given to witness the truth like Jesus Christ did have a great power over others, and over the elements. They have the power "to shut heaven" to stop the rain of comfort on those in whom grace will work out death. They perform great miracles to prove the truth they announce. Note that God gives them this power after they have been brought to nought. The two special witnesses, what power they possess! They shut heaven. They turn the waters of grace and sweetness to blood. All is suffering, misery and strange misfortunes. They smite the weaker ones with all plagues, as often as they will. The heralds of truth have such a great power on others that they are changed inwardly and outwardly under the influence of these two witnesses. If they tell one to have peace, a profound peace comes; and if they do the opposite, then peace is disturbed.

> **Rev. 11:7,8: And when they have finished their testimony, the beast that comes up out of the abyss will make war with them, and overcome them and kill them. And their dead bodies will lie in the street of the great city which mystically is called Sodom and Egypt, where also their Lord was crucified.**

As soon as Jesus Christ had witnessed to the truth, He was smitten by the beast of the pit, for the devil stirred His own to take His life. Those who witness to the truth suffer death. They will positively be killed in the mind of all men. Their bodies shall lie in the world, signifying that there will be no more hope of getting back their reputation. These bodies lie in a spiritual Egypt, in a Sodom where God is not known, where He is dishonored in the strangest way, and in the very place which made my Savior die.

The world is nothing more than Egypt on account of the fighting element and the dislike for harmony and agreement. It is a Sodom on account of disorders and wickedness prevailing there. Shall I tell of those who make up the Church? Catholics and non-Catholics? It seems to me it is a Sodom, this vast variety. The children of God's house dishonor the Church although the Church itself is most holy; but it has been polluted by her children.

The children of the Synagogue crucified their Lord; the children of the Church will kill the faithful witnesses of the truth which abide in the Church. But if they kill them, their bodies will remain out "in the street" to bear witness to this cruelty.

Oh, this is the reign of Satan, this is the time of his efforts to destroy the Church if he can. But it will be in vain; the gates of hell will not prevail against her. Alas, this poor Church is going to remain without comfort! Her children despise and leave her. They lose her Spirit. She carries in her bosom the war between Jacob and Esau. Oh Church, you mourn the loss of your children! Lovely Rachel, you mourn and cannot be comforted because they are not. But cheer up, the time is coming when your children will be brought from all the ends of the earth. You will see them at your table. They will eat your bread and will no longer be rebellious against you. I grant that your children are fighting; within you Esau persecutes Jacob, but soon Jacob will come to life, and as he has been loved by God from eternity, you, too, will love him forever. Rejoice, oh Church, the time of joy is nearing; your grief is going to end. You are going to triumph over everyone and through you Jacob will be victorious. He will prevail with God Who seems to be now against him; and if he keeps limping in the fight, it is only to be a sign, to his seed, of his victory. Jerusalem, holy city — Thy Church — held by the unbelievers for so many years, the time is coming when you will see within your walls the children of the Lord. Jerusalem, you will be the flourishing city!

The beast destroys and kills this witness to the truth for a time, but this is of short duration.

Rev. 11:9,10: **And those from the peoples and tribes and tongues and nations will look at their dead bodies for three and a half days, and will not permit their dead bodies to be laid in a tomb. And those who dwell on the earth will rejoice over them and make merry; and they will send gifts to one another, because these two prophets tormented those who dwell on the earth.**

These two witnesses will be seen and known of all the people on earth, meaning they will be spoken against. All shall rejoice in their apparent defeat. Truth is unbearable, they say. That is why truth is banished from the courts of Princes, from conversations; everybody flees from truth; no one can stand it. Such men always rejoice in their defeat of the two witnesses. But if truth seems defeated for a time it will revive with more strength.

Rev. 11:11–13: **And after the three and a half days the breath of life from God came into them, and they stood on their feet; and great fear fell upon those who were beholding them. And they heard a loud voice from heaven saying to them, "Come up here." And they went up into heaven in the cloud, and their enemies beheld them. And in that hour there was a great earthquake, and a tenth of the city fell; and seven thousand people were killed in the earthquake, and the rest were terrified and gave glory to the God of heaven.**

After three days and a half is the time when truth will seem defeated in this fight. Then the Spirit of life and strength will enter into them.

All those who are intended to bear witness to the truth must have the same fate; they must die, and when they will have been dead for three days and a half – dead to the outward world – a living and quickening Spirit will be sent to them from heaven. After this reviving, they will be received in God Himself. The devil and the flesh will never more be able to attack them.

When it is least expected, God will give them the life that the father of lies had tried to snatch from them. This will be a new life—one that the world cannot receive. Then, after their rising, truth will be completely manifested.

But at the same hour there was a great earthquake. Let us make this an application to those left ... and to their inward parts. They fear destruction; their inferior, or weaker, parts are stripped from their natural life. What once satisfied is taken away. They can not be satisfied by spiritual and divine life, which they never knew.

In this earthquake the tenth part of the city will fall ... a tenth part of the Church will be thrown down. But at the same time seven thousand men will be slain. Oh, unspeakable happiness, soon thereafter sin is destroyed forever. Sin will be banished from the face of the earth, and truth will be known. Oh God, You will not be offended or dishonored anymore! Oh flesh, sin and devil, your empire is going to be destroyed even by the very means you used to establish yourself.

Rev. 11:14: The second woe is past; behold, the third woe is coming quickly.

A "woe" is no longer a woe when it has passed away and very often what seemed to destroy us is the very thing that establishes us. This "woe" was a misfortune only as long as it lasted, but if the time of its duration was troublesome, its consequences are very sweet and agreeable.

Rev. 11:15: And the seventh angel sounded; and there arose loud voices in heaven, saying, "The kingdom of the world has become the kingdom of our Lord, and of His Christ; and He will reign forever and ever."

The opening of the seventh seal showed us the seventh angel announcing unspeakable bliss. Oh pains, works and griefs, how well rewarded you are by the manifestation of the truth! Paul knew this and said the sufferings of this present world are not to be compared with the glory which shall be revealed. Rejoice in your happiness; your tears are wiped. (We must know that all the states that were described take place, more or less, in the inward being of the believer in whom truth has been manifested.)

There is not a word in the book of Revelation that will not happen as it is foretold, not only outwardly but inwardly—in the soul of the believer. The reality of such things will be manifested to all when the seventh seal is open, when the seventh angel will have announced the truth, and it will appear clear and bare as it is.

But what is this truth?

This truth is truly the reign of Jesus Christ outwardly and inwardly.

The souls in whom Jesus Christ reigns absolutely will be placed in reality. The outer reign of Jesus Christ will extend throughout all the world. But as He will extend outwardly, so He will also be extended inwardly. The same century that is fortunate enough to see everyone subject to the reign of Jesus Christ, will also see every heart on earth under His control and will. All will follow the moves of His Spirit. Then shall the will of God be done on earth as in Heaven. He will reign in the minds and hearts forever and ever.

> **Rev. 11:16,17: And the twenty-four elders, who sit on their thrones before God, fell on their faces and worshiped God, saying, "We give Thee thanks, O Lord God, the Almighty, who art and who wast, because Thou hast taken Thy great power and hast begun to reign."**

Nothing will gladden more the holy ones (and Heaven) as the time in which the reign of Jesus Christ must spread throughout the earth. Before this time, Jesus Christ had all power given Him in Heaven and on earth; but He chose that His power would be spread only when it is exercised in the hearts and minds of all men. That is why it is written, "The Lord said to my Lord: Sit down at my right hand till I make your enemies your footstool."

This happens when all rebellious wills come under Him.

Then shall everyone be moved and led by Him. This is the joy of the blessed ones and the greatest glory that God can receive from His creatures.

> **Rev. 11:18,19: "And the nations were enraged, and Thy wrath came, and the time came for the dead to be judged, and the time to give their reward to**

**Thy bond-servants the prophets and to the saints
and to those who fear Thy name, the small and the
great, and to destroy those who destroy the earth."
And the temple of God which is in heaven was
opened; and the ark of His covenant appeared in
His temple, and there were flashes of lightning and
sounds and peals of thunder and an earthquake
and a great hailstorm.**

After John spoke of the marvelous reign of Jesus
Christ he is shown another scene. The nations will seem to
become angry against the reign of Jesus Christ. Those who
will be most opposed in feelings will agree to persecute this
reign and destroy the inward way. Their fury will be stirred.
It seems God will give them some power to destroy. But
then the day of the wrath of God comes; He takes vengeance on the enemies of His reign (and of the inward life) and
He punishes them in an amazing way.

Then comes the time of judging the dead, that is, judging those who died spiritually . . . having suffered a thousand deaths through the cruelty of men who stole their
honor. After having been oppressed a long time, God's justice will have it known to all that they were in the truth, not
their enemies. Then will God "reward the prophets," showing the truth of the words they spoke. He will show that the
way they followed was the true way for all.

Two things corrupted the earth, the carnal mind and
self will. They opposed the reign of Jesus Christ constantly.
The fleshly mind led to idolatry and self will is the source
of all other sins. So Jesus Christ will not absolutely and
entirely reign on earth unless these two enemies are
destroyed. That is why He has raised two powerful enemies
against the carnal mind and self will: faith and pure love.
To establish faith and pure love in place of the fleshly mind
and the self is the purpose of God in sending the two witnesses.

When that time comes, the temple of God will be
opened. All nations will enter in the Church of God. Then
the ark of His testament will be seen. (That is to say, the
wonderful ways He used, and is using, to unite Himself to
men.) Oh God, how many truths You will uncover to Your
poor creatures when Your truth is manifested! But this will
happen only after the thunderings, noises, and lightnings

strike the powers which now are rendering God a service by opposing His kingdom!

When the time comes and their eyes open, they will be very surprised to see they fought the truth thinking they were fighting a lie.

Paul is an example of what will then happen. Those who will have fought the truth with the greatest zeal, will defend it with the greatest strength.

12

Rev. 12:1,2: And a great sign appeared in heaven: a woman clothed with the sun, and the moon under her feet, and on her head a crown of twelve stars; and she was with child; and she cried out, being in labor and in pain to give birth.

This woman has two distinct meanings, all of them very true.

One is that the depths of knowing our Lord must be born on earth. It was always in Heaven, but has not been produced on earth. The Spirit of truth has been somewhat banished. Reality must come back on earth, produced by pure love. The second meaning is that the Church wants to give birth to this truth (which comes only by the inner way).

This woman, according to these two meanings, is surrounded with the "Sun," that is by truth, manifested in this life. She has the moon under her feet because she is above unstableness and wavering. When the soul of the believer is established in the truth, it does not change any more in its foundation. That is why this one has the moon under her feet.

She is clothed with the sun; she is above all changeable and varying lights. She has a crown of twelve stars, the twelve fruits of the Holy Spirit. The soul that has truly known Him deeply possesses them all. This one has joy, peace, patience, longsuffering, etc. When Reality is on earth, love reigns. Where truth is, there is also love.

She is with child and wants to produce her fruit in the

world. This fruit is righteousness. Jesus Christ produced righteousness on the cross and His grief was extreme. What pain must be known to produce such righteousness! The inner walk must produce righteousness, just as — counterwise — lies produced unrighteousness. Up till the time of this scene, unrighteousness reigns on earth, because its father, Lying, brought it there. This is why men steal from God His glory. They consider as belonging to themselves what should be attributed to God only. From this unrighteousness brought about through lies came all evils we have on earth. But as soon as Reality has produced righteousness, men give back to God what they owe Him.

The second explanation of this woman is that she is the Church.

The Church is about to give birth to the inner Spirit: her true Spirit. She is with child, possessing this Spirit which is like a second advent of Jesus Christ. She is in pains to be delivered for it will cost her sufferings; the fruit will be precious and more good must be produced; suffering is, therefore, unquestionable.

It seems that this Spirit remained enclosed within her. (Some have been stirred and partook of the divine revelation Paul explained but this has been very rare.) All Christians have been called to this; but they did not all answer the call. On the contrary, these Christians opposed the inner way. As the Church is about to spread out her branches, she wants to produce her Spirit in all her members. This is the spirit of abandonment, and divine moving, so fought against today.

Rev. 12:3,4: And another sign appeared in heaven: and behold, a great red dragon having seven heads and ten horns, and on his heads were seven diadems. And his tail swept away a third of the stars of heaven, and threw them to the earth. And the dragon stood before the woman who was about to give birth, so that when she gave birth he might devour her child.

This "Dragon" is self love, the father of the lie. He is opposed to pure love; he is the mortal enemy of truth, and even in Heaven wished to prefer himself to God, wanting to attribute to himself that which is due to God only.

This Dragon, in the Garden of Eden, instilled his poison in man and having withdrawn man from truth, caused man to be chased away. This same Dragon, today, seeing that the inner Reality is going to come to light in the world, is standing firm to devour it and to hinder its appearing on earth. It must be known that inner reality produces pure love and that pure love brings righteousness to life.

This righteousness just means snatching everything from the creature and giving all to God! As soon as the soul is so endowed,?

This Dragon is "red" because he apes pure love. The seven heads are the totality of deadly sins in the world. The ten horns represent the transgression of the law. These seven heads are crowned to indicate that this Dragon reigns in the world through the sin which he introduced.

This Dragon draws with its tail the third part of men. Through shrewdness he makes most of them fall, disclosing his hatred only after he draws them because he uses subtlety and craftiness. This horrible Dragon "stands before this woman who was going to be delivered to devour her child." Self love produces unrighteousness and devours righteousness, preventing God from receiving His due and upsetting the order of things. This is why this horrible Dragon, this Lucifer, had so many everywhere worshipping him. When he sees that this righteousness which he had thought that he had banished was returning, then he does all in his power to devour the fruit and swallow the mother.

The Church is ready to bring to life this inner Spirit. Now that the Church wants to show and reproduce in the whole Universe this Spirit, enclosed within her, she is in "pains"; she cannot help speaking of her grief, though no one knows the cause of it and they attribute it to other things. This dragon is constantly before her to devour her fruit in his birth; but how useless will his efforts be! Truth will triumph over the lie, pure love over self-love, righteousness over unrighteousness.

Rev. 12:5,6: And she gave birth to a son, a male child, who is to rule all the nations with a rod of

iron; and her child was caught up to God and to His throne. And the woman fled into the wilderness where she had a place prepared by God, so that there she might be nourished for one thousand two hundred and sixty days.

She fails not in producing her fruit, as it had been seen and foretold by David in Psalm 85:10.

This Fruit will govern the nations with a rod of iron. Not one will oppose Him; all people will worship the true God. They will rightly honor Him by the means of submitting their mind to the truth. They will submit their heart to His wonderful leading.

"This son was caught up unto God" because God will Himself preserve the righteousness which the nations must have for Him.

He will be on "the throne" of God; all nations will acknowledge Him as their God, as the one in whom is enclosed all power and all merit, whom they must adore, to whom they must be led unreservedly and abandon their heart and mind completely.

This woman is banished to the wilderness, to a solitary place ... to hearts prepared for her. But Reality must be hidden there, that no one may find it. She will be cared for "a thousand two hundred and sixty days." Oh, mysteries truer than the daylight, you are regarded now as fables and tales for children, as daydreams. You will appear in all your splendor and these words will be considered only with respect. Then people will see they come from God. They have been written by the command of my God. You will appear one day. You will be placed on the seashore as a lighthouse reaching all the travelers with its light. Oh despised Truth, You Who are hated on earth, You will be their admiration, beauty and light.

This flight into the wilderness means that only emptied hearts will receive this woman of truth. From there, faith will spread out. There is a semblance of faith, pictures of faith. However as this faith will never be withdrawn from earth, God chose for it a wilderness where it will be cared for.

Oh dragon, all your efforts to engulf this Spirit of faith are useless; God protects it in such a special way that it is kept near Him, to be spread out on the earth after you are bound. Then that which was the abomination of the earth will be its glory and stay!

Rev. 12:7: And there was war in heaven, Michael and his angels waging war with the dragon. And the dragon and his angels waged war, ...

This war "in heaven" is the war of self-love against pure love. Michael is the angel of love, and will protect those who are placed in love. This is a very strange and rough fight. This is why the soul is like a heaven where this fight takes place and suffers greatly. The dragon defends himself with all his might; this wretched self-love (which seemed to leave the soul in peace when no one disturbed him), now gives such fierce blows that there is no fight as tough as this in this world. This is the last fight of all. Michael uses all his weapons to fight self-love. This wretched dragon uses all he has to defend himself. Oh, terrible and frightful attacks!

This fight took place in Heaven at the creation of the world; it takes place now in the Church and in the soul of every believer who is meant to receive the pure love. Now Michael and the followers of inner love fight with all their might. This dragon defends himself as well as he can, but inner love will conquer, after strange wars.

Rev. 12:8: ... and they were not strong enough, and there was no longer a place found for them in heaven.

Oh, self-love, arm yourself as much as it pleases you to fight. You will remain the weakest.

In the same manner, with the individual soul, as soon as self-love is defeated. But, oh God, how long, what sufferings, what fight before it is defeated!

Rev. 12:9: And the great dragon was thrown down, the serpent of old who is called the devil and Satan, who deceives the whole world; he was thrown down to the earth, and his angels were thrown down with him.

It is a sure fact that as soon as self-love is entirely destroyed and that inner and pure love takes its place, the devil is cast out and has no longer any power over the soul. As soon as self-love has disappeared, there is no more grip of the devil.

Likewise when this war, a pure and inner love against self-love, comes to an end, the dragon will have no more power on the servants of God. He is going to be chased out and the prince of this world will soon be destroyed. The victory Jesus Christ won over him will have its complete result.

> **Rev. 12:10: And I heard a loud voice in heaven, saying, "Now the salvation, and the power, and the kingdom of our God and the authority of His Christ have come, for the accuser of our brethren has been thrown down, who accuses them before our God day and night."**

Joy beyond words is in Heaven when this power is broken. The soul that is free from loving itself finds no longer the accuser in its own conscience.

Your Lord requires that we should ask for His kingdom to come; but this kingdom could not come before His will would be fully done on earth as it is in heaven. The will of God is perfectly done in heaven when self-love is dispelled.

As soon as this will is done the whole Church of God, the heavenly and earthly Church, sings with all her might. Now is come salvation ... which means salvation is firm and sure. Salvation was not universal, for numberless souls, drawn by the dragon's tail, fell into the pit, but as soon as he is knocked down and chased out, the kingdom of God is established. Man is no longer strong in his own strength, but God's strength is in him. The tempter is no longer. Here is a state of innocence which is the fruit and redemption of Jesus Christ — such an abundant redemption that those who taste the fruit of it are astounded.

Here appears the time of the "strength" of our God. Now, oh God, You are going to be king and reign sovereignly. Your reign will however be a reign of peace, full of delights. Now, in this scene, You are reigning! Now the power of Jesus Christ and the result of His death appear. Oh God, it seemed You had no power and that the devil had an almost unmastered power because he was strengthened by self-love. But now Your power appears because self-love is put aside. Oh salvation, how great you are! This day will happen without fail. There is not a man on earth who will not bend his knees before You.

> **Rev. 12:11,12: "And they overcame him because of the blood of the Lamb and because of the word of their testimony, and they did not love their life even to death. For this reason, rejoice, O heavens and you who dwell in them. Woe to the earth and the sea, because the devil has come down to you, having great wrath, knowing that he has only a short time."**

The dragon (self-love) is conquered only by the blood of the Lamb and the word of their testimony about Jesus Christ. Just as heaven is free, so there is no more admission for the devil and self-love into this highest part of the soul. And even for the lower parts, deliverance is near.

The devil is now banished from the heavenlies and falls on the earth where he will exercise his cruelty for a short time; he does this with so much tyranny that it seems the world must perish. So in our souls, as long as self-love rules, pure love is nearly gone, living only in some solitary places, in some few chosen souls.

The dragon exercises his cruelty with more strength than ever. But if desolation is great, we rejoice because the time of deliverance is near. Oh, if the souls on which the dragon pours his hatred with so much fury understood that deliverance is near! What joy they would have! But they are persecuted and are persuaded that this time will never end. However, it will end soon and unexpectedly.

> **Rev. 12:13,14: And when the dragon saw that he was thrown down to the earth, he persecuted the woman who gave birth to the male child. And the two wings of the great eagle were given to the woman, in order that she might fly into the wilderness to her place, where she was nourished for a time and times and half a time, from the presence of the serpent.**

The dragon wars against the truth the most cruel war there ever was. It seems all men are against the reality of

Christ. But the wings of an eagle are given this one and she flies into the wilderness, with the souls separated from the world, where deception has not come. Separated from the world there she is fed – helped – for the future day of her appearance.

The Church will never be more "persecuted" than by her own children. Nor will the individual believer. She will "fly" in places where she was not known. There she will be known. This spirit of faith and truth, the inner spirit, its ornament, will be hidden for a while; then will come a time when these deeper things will appear in all their beauty.

Rev. 12:15,16: And the serpent poured water like a river out of his mouth after the woman, so that he might cause her to be swept away with the flood. And the earth helped the woman, and the earth opened its mouth and drank up the river which the dragon poured out of his mouth.

This "flood" that the serpent casts out is deceit. He wants to swallow reality by this horrible flood; he believes that truth will not be able to withstand the flood of lies. But earth opens up to swallow this horrible flood. Floods are thrown against the Church (and the inward believer), fighting her spirit under the pretext of sustaining her doctrine. (Only you, oh Jesus, know the malice of these people, covered with sheep skin but within, they are ravening wolves.) The dragon uses them, vomiting his flood of self-love, his poison, to engulf the spirit of the Church, and the inner spirit, but his efforts will be in vain.

Rev. 12:17: And the dragon was enraged with the woman, and went off to make war with the rest of her offspring, who keep the commandments of God and hold to the testimony of Jesus.

The dragon, seeing he can do nothing against the Church and the Truth, goes to make war with her children. He stirs up a general persecution against all the inner souls who love the truth. They will suffer by him in many ways. Only the true children of truth are molested. They have the testimony of Jesus Christ which is really the reign of Jesus Christ within them.

13

Rev. 13:1: And he stood on the sand of the sea-shore. And I saw a beast coming up out of the sea, having ten horns and seven heads, and on his horns were ten diadems, and on his heads were blasphemous names.

This frightful monster is produced by self-love in the believer, waging everlasting war against all men. This is the pride of life. This beast rises up "out of the sea," for it appears on this stormy sea of life. This war is more open than the preceding; however it is almost the same thing. He has "seven heads," that is to say, seven sprouts that are a part of him as is his self-love. His "ten horns" are ambition, hatred, jealousy, the contempt of others, slander, unrighteousness, murders, quarrellings, usurpation, luxury, revenge, ungodliness. These ten horns are crowned, for there is not one for which a crown is not given. Ambition is called honor; hatred and jealousy are signs of intelligence and discernment; the rest are said to come from a great heart or a fine soul! Each of these horns has its crown, its sanction; no one admits he is proud ... only courageous.

Upon his heads is the name of blasphemy, appropriating to himself what belongs to God; he dishonors Him, blasphemes Him, shamelessly offends Him. Nothing is more opposed to God than self-interest and pride. If God could be dethroned, it would be done by His creature, just to take His place.

Rev. 13:2: And the beast which I saw was like a leopard, and his feet were like those of a bear, and his mouth like the mouth of a lion. And the dragon gave him his power and his throne and great authority.

The leopard is very beautiful outwardly and his skin is beautiful. It is like self-interest, covered with the finest appearance; its outward part charms. But his feet were as of a bear, to rise above all that opposes his own reign. His feet are very ugly, completely opposed to what he shows outside. His mouth is as the mouth of a lion because he devours everything. All is used to feed him—the poor, the widow, the orphan, the seeking soul, all are devoured by him and are his food and support.

The dragon gave him his power. All the might and malice of the devil is enclosed in pride, the eldest son of self-interest!

A soul without pride is a soul in the state of nothingness in whom the devil has no more power. Pride is, therefore, the head of all sins and it is the source of sin, just as pure love is the headwaters of truth. Self-love is both the son and the father of pride, and pure love is the source of all virtues. He who possesses an inner love cannot be controlled by sin although it seems to him that he does not have any virtue.

Rev. 13:3: And I saw one of his heads as if it had been slain, and his fatal wound was healed. And the whole earth was amazed and followed after the beast; ...

Sometimes it seems to the seeking believer that some vice has been destroyed and some head brought down, but when it seems dead, then it rises with more violence and fury. All vices continue to be renewed till self-interest is entirely destroyed.

The whole earth wondered, because love for self and ambition are desired by all men (even the most spiritual ones).

Where will we find a man who does not seek his own interest? The Scripture says: "All seek their own." Only those who seek the interest of God alone, do good. Will someone be found who has no interest except God's? The priest chooses the priesthood out of self-interest. The preacher will preach for God's glory; however he seeks his own glory and applause. The missionary seeks success. But those who do not look at themselves in any way, who, when forsaken by all, even forsaken of God, do not look at themselves but at the interest of God alone, how rare!

> **Rev. 13:4,5,6:** . . . **and they worshiped the dragon, because he gave his authority to the beast; and they worshiped the beast, saying, "Who is like the beast, and who is able to wage war with him?" And there was given to him a mouth speaking arrogant words and blasphemies; and authority to act for forty-two months was given to him. And he opened his mouth in blasphemies against God, to blaspheme His name and His tabernacle, that is, those who dwell in heaven.**

All men who still live in themselves are idolaters of self-interest. And since self-interest gets its power from self-love, their fate is the same; if you destroy one, you cannot do otherwise than destroy the other; and if you idolize one, you will the other.

Those who are possessed by this spirit of self-interest and self-love, who worship the beast, say there is nothing like their way of acting. Who can resist their motives and prudence? They glory in their success and in the applause given by all.

Power was given unto him to continue forty and two months oppressing God's servants. These people rise with a frightful boldness. They blaspheme His name, considering the anointing of His grace to be an error.

These people have the impertinence to condemn what they are not fortunate enough to feel. (These graces are never granted to those who go after self-interest and self-love). They blaspheme against the inward life, and "against those that dwell" in God.

The tabernacle of God is inward. God lives and makes His abode in the whole soul as He promised to do for those who will do His will. Nearly all men rave against this tabernacle; they cannot stand that God be worshiped in this tabernacle.

Rev. 13:7: And it was given to him to make war with the saints and to overcome them; and authority over every tribe and people and tongue and nation was given to him.

Self-interest wages a continuous war against the saints who have suffered to be stripped of all so as to give glory and homage to the majesty of God. It seems the whole earth is armed against these saints and always wins the battle. (Those who are back of this triumph are said to be saints, great ones, while the saints themselves are defeated, oppressed, and undone). The saints will eventually be withdrawn from oppression and God will give them back what they lost and much compensation besides. However all the rest of mankind will be overcome and possessed by this spirit of self-interest.

Rev. 13:8: And all who dwell on the earth will worship him, everyone whose name has not been written from the foundation of the world in the book of life of the Lamb who has been slain.

Only true, inward believers, marked with the seal of the Lamb, do not serve self-love and greed. Those who have the nature of the Lamb seek the Lamb only. Vices have taken the names of virtues. Virtues such as pure love, naked faith, hope which has no stay, complete denial, true humility, all these virtues are considered evils and vices. Everybody agrees to condemn virtues. However these are essential virtues without which we have only the name and appearance of a Christian. We can be comforted that no matter how great corruption is, there will also be many inner persons who belong to God, with the seal of the Lamb, and having His nature.

This Lamb was slain from the foundation of the world, which means from the beginning of the inner Christian world, for it was in this sacrifice and in the blood of this Lamb without spot that the world received a new life. This Lamb, by His sacrifice, changed the book of death into "a book of life" by the efficacy of His blood. The Lamb, by His sacrifice, redeemed us from death, and had this condemnation of death changed into a promise of life. As soon as the soul allows Jesus Christ to do the living of the believer – from within – that believer is sealed with His seal and nature. Self-love and self-interest have no power over these souls because they are freed from tyranny by the blood of Jesus Christ and submit to His power. However, those who do not have His seal, the Beast has power over them.

What is it to be a Christian? "They have crucified the flesh" (Gal. 5:24).

A "new creature ... old things have passed away, all things have become new" (2 Cor. 5).

"All those who are baptized into Jesus Christ are baptized into His death" (Rom. 6).

"As many as are led by the Spirit, they are the sons of God" (Rom. 8).

Those who are Christians in this manner are marked with the seal of the Lamb!

Rev. 13:9,10: If anyone has an ear, let him hear. If anyone is destined for captivity, to captivity he goes; if anyone kills with the sword, with the sword he must be killed. Here is the perseverance and the faith of the saints.

Those who attack an inwardly living one and cause such a one to suffer should fear this passage. They succeed, for awhile, because God allows them to. The believing ones, as a result, become gold in the furnace of humiliation. But after God has used these persecutors to purify His servants and bring them to nought, He punishes the antagonist who chastised His children.

Let those who triumph against us today be persuaded that they will some day be led into captivity, and that the same evils they put on others are waiting for them.

My God, sometimes You seem to have no eyes or ears; but a time comes when You know how to avenge Your servants.

As for you, oh servants of God, rejoice in your oppression, be exceedingly glad, because you must show your faithfulness to God. This is only to prove your faith. God tries you as He did Abraham to see if you will not lose your faithfulness when you are oppressed, afflicted and tormented.

91

Rev. 13:11,12: And I saw another beast coming up out of the earth; and he had two horns like a lamb, and he spoke as a dragon. And he exercises all the authority of the first beast in his presence. And he makes the earth and those who dwell in it to worship the first beast, whose fatal wound was healed.

This beast is "carnality." This beast is not any less dangerous than the other two; on the contrary, the danger of this beast is less apparent, and this is why it is more harmful. Why? This one retains goodness. Its appearance is very beautiful. It is full of its own righteousness, but in such a hidden way that it cannot be discerned because it has two horns like a lamb.

The horns of the true lamb are righteousness and divine strength. This beast's horns are self-righteousness and self-strength. That is why he comes out of the earth — because he comes from the corrupt nature while the Lamb comes from above. How can we know this frightful monster? By his voice. The speech of the Word is always fruitful, seeking the glory of God. But this beast seeks only his own glory and benefit.

This frightful beast "exercises all the power of the first beast" (the tyranny of self-interest). He has this self-interest worshipped and adored more because he is backed up by covetousness (the power to possess).

Rev, 13:13: And he performs great signs, so that he even makes fire come down out of heaven to the earth in the presence of men.

Carnality covered by an appearance of godliness is so powerful that it makes fire come down from heaven. It has the power to inspire some apparent conversion, but this is not lasting. The devil gives the feelings of certain passing fires which seem to come from heaven and help the swelling pride of this beast, giving it a new hold on men.

If a man with carnality starts anything, he will succeed. Success swells and develops a sense of carnality. Failure brings a sense of nothingness and need of God.

Rev. 13:14: And he deceives those who dwell on the earth because of the signs which it was given him

to perform in the presence of the beast, telling those who dwell on the earth to make an image to the beast who had the wound of the sword and has come to life.

This carnality (covetousness) deceives them that dwell on the earth. This means those who live in themselves who are sure of themselves. This beast blinds them so that they are persuaded that good is evil and evil good. It entices them to make an image of the beast. This image is a likeness of self-love which is said to be the love of God because self-love imitates pure love. The image of self-love seems to be a pure love to those who have no understanding.

This beast has a wound. This wound does not make him die though it is a deadly wound. Love of self lives in the very things which would cause others to die. Here is the difference between self-love and pure love: He who has pure love dies truly because of the wounds he has received, while self-love becomes more alive by them. The world is deceived and blind to this. These are idols, not pastors, and they are idolized.

This idolatry comes about because of carnality.

Rev. 13:15: And there was given to him to give breath to the image of the beast, that the image of the beast might even speak and cause as many as do not worship the image of the beast to be killed.

He who is not indwelt by the Spirit of God is moved with carnality which is worshipped, now, everywhere. Today carnality has the right to speak to whomever it pleases. It alone now draws attention; some good souls only are excepted for they understand the language of pure love. The rest understand only the language of the beast; the language of pure love seems strange and harsh. The Spirit of the Church and of the Gospel appears peculiar and suspicious to them. As for the language of the beast, everybody understands it. It comes naturally to all. This carnality is so foreign to the pure love that little by little it destroys divine love. And so, carnality oppresses those who do not submit to self-love, which in itself is a god.

Oh, truth clearer than the daylight, why are you not understood?

Rev. 13:16: And he causes all, the small and the great, and the rich and the poor, and the free men and the slaves, to be given a mark on their right hand, or on their forehead, ...

Self-interest is stirring everyone to act in our day. All on the earth are led by it. This is "the mark" all receive from the beast ... they only think of themselves and for themselves; they will act for themselves and by themselves! All men act thus! (Except those who have the mark of the Lamb ... they have no other interest besides that of God alone. This is their mark.

The characteristic and mark of the servants of God is this: God alone in everything, God and His cross. No more thought for self but God alone, His glory only, His interest alone! Speak to this soul of anything you like, wealth, honors, life, friends, children, salvation, eternity, perfection – he does not know any other language but: God alone. He consults only God in all undertakings. This is the seal and characteristic of the Lamb. Others have to consult their own interest or the interest of honor, glory, reputation, family, money, promotion. Self-interest is then the mark and language of the beast.

Rev. 13:18: Here is wisdom. Let him who has understanding calculate the number of the beast, for the number is that of a man; and his number is six hundred and sixty-six.

It is said that those who love Him only and passionately are not adapted to their environment; they are not qualified for business, because it is said they do not know how to lie or deceive. But oh God, the truth is they are hated by the world because they are not of it and do not have the mark of it. They are not like other men, for they are marked with the mark of Jesus Christ. Although they are the meekest and kindest of men, they are avoided, feared, hated as if they were scoundrels. Oh, hostile condemnation!

Wherever souls are marked with the characteristics of Jesus Christ, they will be speaking the same language, acting in the same way; likewise those who bear the characteristics of the beast speak and act like the beast. Here is wisdom ... to know how to discern the characteristics of the beast and those of Jesus Christ.

14

Rev. 14:1: And I looked, and behold, the Lamb was standing on Mount Zion, and with Him one hundred and forty-four thousand, having His name and the name of His Father written on their foreheads.

"The Lamb stood on Mount Zion."

I see this, in Reality, as the Lord standing at the center of a man's soul. He dwells there, where He delights to be, in the soul marked with His seal and with His characteristics engraved on it. Those marked with His seal are a hundred forty-four thousand; they are united among themselves, being of like feelings, speaking the same language, acting alike. These souls are always "with the Lamb," Who indwells them.

Just as the Lamb is at the center of the believer's being, He is also at the center of the Church. These souls are in a continual nothingness, sharing in His continual sacrifice. Oh, happy souls who in a dissolute world have the joy of belonging to Jesus Christ! You are hidden, dead, and nothing, suffering offenses, shame and slander, like Him, in perfect silence. But a time is coming when you will rise from your shame and nothingness, to have a part in the marriage supper of the Lamb, having been made worthy.

Rev. 14:2,3: And I heard a voice from heaven, like the sound of many waters and like the sound of loud thunder, and the voice which I heard was like the sound of harpists playing on their harps. And

they sang a new song before the throne and before the four living creatures and the elders; and no one could learn the song except the one hundred and forty-four thousand who had been purchased from the earth.

This voice is the voice of surrendering souls. It is the voice of harpers; it is a complete harmony, a continuous accord of every will submitted to the will of God. This is the cause of their perfect harmony. They are all moved by the same spirit and have only one undivided will—God's will.

These souls sing a new song, and no man could learn that song nor understand it, for it will only be understood by souls emptied of self, enjoying a divine language from God alone. It is "new" because no one else ever sang it or can sing it. They could sing it only after they were completely stripped and "redeemed from the earth." They have been redeemed from all the earthly in Adam.

Rev. 14:4: These are the ones who have not been defiled with women, for they have kept themselves chaste. These are the ones who follow the Lamb wherever He goes. These have been purchased from among men as first fruits to God and to the Lamb.

There is "a virginity" of the soul in keeping the grace of God. A soul that is perfectly free from earthly things is a virgin soul. The Adam in them is completely destroyed. These follow the Lamb wherever He goes. They cannot part from Him because of the unity that their nothingness has accomplished. But if such people have noted advantages, oh God, what crosses also do they bear!

These are redeemed from among men, that is, withdrawn from all human corruption in their nature—self-love, and carnality. They are also the first fruits to God, specially sacrificed to Him. As soon as these souls are withdrawn from the world, they dwell in the bosom of God. Fiery flames, impurities, carnality are all gone.

Rev. 14:5: And no lie was found in their mouth; they are blameless.

In their mouth was found no guile; their words are the very truth since they show the completeness of God and the nothingness of creature. They are like a spotless mirror in which the Sun of righteousness likes to be reflected and continually see Himself.

Rev. 14:6: And I saw another angel flying in midheaven, having an eternal gospel to preach to those who live on the earth, and to every nation and tribe and tongue and people; ...

The eternal gospel is only the will of God which was and always will be. It is the gospel of truth unknown of all men. Oh God, create men who will obey You perfectly, men who will never rebel in any place You put them. This is the everlasting gospel, for eternally Your will was accomplished very perfectly. You did Your will in Yourself; then in Your angels.

This eternal gospel is that of God's will preached to all the earth. It will be preached. It is hardly known now. It will be the common and universal language. Oh divine Language, you will be the delight of men on earth! What made man miserable was his disobedience. What will make man happy will be the fulfillment of God's will. Man will never be perfectly happy even if he were to possess the whole world, without doing God's will. The least resistance brings a worldly man trouble, suffering, grief. As soon as he does what God wants him to do, he comes into peace and unspeakable joy.

And it is by this very circumstance that he can know whether he is yielding or resisting God. We fail to do God's will because we judge this will with our reasonings, thoughts, human feelings, the hearsay of men, their self-love and self-interest. In judging this way, we do not enter into this will. Let us judge it through abandonment, self-denial in everything, through all God is doing and allowing, through what gives peace, joy, freedom.

Rev. 14:7: ... and he said with a loud voice, "Fear God, and give Him glory, because the hour of His judgment has come; and worship Him who made the heaven and the earth and sea and springs of waters."

Nearly everyone believes that the fear of God is being afraid of punishment. But this is fear born of self-love, not that of pure love. The fear of pure love is this: that we will not please God enough or do His will. The soul is here invited to give glory to Him for the hour of His judgment is come. The soul who has no self-interest or self-love will love His judgment however severe it may be, because God thus justifies Himself against His creature who, unjustly having robbed God, withdrew from God – and His will – to do his own.

Oh Love, fulfill Your judgment. Whatever it is, I love it. It will make You glorious and that will suffice. Your Glory alone, oh God, is my delight.

All Christians believe they worship God but it would be easy to prove that very few worship Him. Worshipping God inwardly is paying homage to His sovereignty by being nothing without Him. Worshipping God outwardly is having a profound respect in His presence. But this outward worship cannot be true unless it is backed by the inward. Who is nothing before God? Who stands before God both with the humility and respect due to Him? Christians who go into a church building on Sunday are like in a market place or in a fair. No one would think we believe in a present God. Lack of reverence in the Church will be severely punished. Turks and heathens have a thousand times more respect in their temples!

Rev. 14:8: And another angel, a second one, followed, saying, "Fallen, fallen is Babylon the great, she who has made all the nations drink of the wine of the passion of her immorality."

"Babylon" is a city of confusion, greed, pride, sensualism. This Babylon is self-will, the daughter of pride. Since God wants to establish his everlasting Gospel, which is His will, He must destroy and bring down self-will. Every sin begins when we separate our will from God's. Adam brought sin into the world because his will was contrary to God's. If our will was united to God's, we would never sin.

God must then bring down this self-will before establishing the everlasting Gospel. This is how He works with souls: He starts by having them lose their own will; then He substitutes His own there.

This is not done at once; creature could not stand it. It is done little by little, God bearing with our weakness.

This Babylon made all nations drink of the wine of the wrath of her fornication.

We even do our own will when we have to obey men. Scripture rightly calls this "fornication," because our own will was created to be united to God's and be one with God. However, the soul withdrew from God to obey the devil. Since then it has been in continuous rebellion. Man withdrew himself from the unity and simplicity of God to enter the multiplicity of Babylon.

Rev. 14:9,10: And another angel, a third one, followed them, saying with a loud voice, "If anyone worships the beast and his image, and receives a mark on his forehead or upon his hand, he also will drink of the wine of the wrath of God, which is mixed in full strength in the cup of His anger; and he will be tormented with fire and brimstone in the presence of the holy angels and in the presence of the Lamb."

The chastisement of those who are marked with the seal and characteristics of self-interest could not be too great. They rejected the sacred fire of the purest love to be burned with the fire of greed. They called their own love, pure love and called pure love, self-love, thus blaspheming the Holy Spirit and doing their own corrupt and unrestrained will. They placed the mark of the beast on their forehead – on their mind – which is filled with themselves, their business, pleasures, glory, covetousness. They received also the mark "in their hand," dedicating all their works to the service of their self-interest and carnality.

This is why they do not want to drink of the wine of the Bridegroom's cellars. He gives it to souls willing to be emptied of themselves.

But these others reject this pure love. Just as pure love, this strong and delicious wine fills with peace and joy him who drinks of it, so that it fully quenches his thirst; likewise the other who drinks His wine is filled with trouble and grief.

Man had been created to love his God. His love had to make man happy, and satisfy him fully. Instead of this, man allowed the poison of the serpent to slip into his heart; this strange love became his tormentor. It leaves man thirsty forever. The torment they have in this world is very weak in comparison with what they will suffer hereafter; it will be a continuation and an increase of evil.

Gross, carnal sins rightly frighten us; these which are monsters a thousand times more frightful do not cause us to fear. On the contrary, they are continued on, loved, pampered, tolerated as if they were insignificant. Are there in the world beasts as frightful as those described here? Nevertheless other animals are feared which are easily tamed, but this horrible monster which causes such great misfortunes is revered.

Oh, blindness! The light of the truth is done away with, hidden in the desert, in barren, solitary places, devoted to pure love. Men walk in the light of a false illumination, dazzled without enlightenment, seeing cliffs as if they were mountains and the mountains as if they were cliffs. Oh, God, send Your light of truth! You will, oh Love, when the dragon is killed and destroyed, and when Babylon is entirely knocked down.

Rev. 14:11: "And the smoke of their torment goes up forever and ever; and they have no rest day and night, those who worship the beast and his image, and whoever receives the mark of his name."

Those who worship the beast have in them an apparent and deadly sense of carnality. Oh God, Your sacred fire will know how to try everything, reject what is impure and against You, and purify what is Yours. It is certain that these greedy, important people suffer and are tormented in this very life. for they have no rest day and night. But the torments awaiting them in the hereafter are stranger still. The servants of God go through many crosses, troubles and afflictions, but these bring about in the sufferer a certain deep peace. When the outward life is most desolate, the inward enjoys a deeper satisfaction. It is said that to be saved you must go through a great deal of suffering; but personally I find that you must go through far more suffering to get lost.

100

Rev. 14:12: Here is the perseverance of the saints who keep the commandments of God and their faith in Jesus.

Believers need great patience to live with sinners who torment them constantly. Everybody sees their interests and sides with them, but they condemn God's servants. These things will change. Do not grow weary suffering persecution. God acts in this manner to give you a better crown by sending troubles now to exercise your "patience." He increases your patience by the measure of the cross He sends, and you become hardened against suffering. This patience is given to those who continue in the will of God and place their trust in Jesus Christ.

Rev. 14:13: And I heard a voice from heaven, saying, "Write, 'Blessed are the dead who die in the Lord from now on!'" "Yes," says the Spirit, "that they may rest from their labors, for their deeds follow with them."

My God, what beautiful words! How comforting! There are two kinds of deaths in the Lord. To die the first death in the Lord, man must die to himself in all he has from Adam, all that is outward, human and possessing him. Oh, happy death indeed that sweeps away all pains. Oh, blessed death, bringing the soul out of itself and into God. Oh death, beginning of true life! Oh, blessed death by which the soul is lost in God! After this death, the natural death is a wonderful happiness. Through it we enjoy God perfectly and clearly with the veil of faith. Without this death, the natural death is something which is feared.

"Indifference" to all that life holds is spoken of by Paul in Romans 14: "Whether we live therefore or die, we are the Lord's." Such believers would not stay if they were not meant to help others. However they are ready to remain on earth indefinitely.

Rev. 14:14,15: And I looked, and behold, a white cloud, and sitting on the cloud was one like a son of man, having a golden crown on His head, and a

sharp sickle in His hand. And another angel came out of the temple, crying out with a loud voice to Him who sat on the cloud, "Put in your sickle and reap, because the hour to reap has come, because the harvest of the earth is ripe."

The Lord Jesus must reap the harvest. You gave Your life so as to change the tares sown by the enemy into good seeds from the purest wheat. However these tares wanted to save their own nature in spite of Your care and goodness. You will reap them with Your sharp sickle and take to Yourself the good grain. You will throw the other into the fire.

Some souls are ripe for heaven, as the others are ripe for hell.

Rev. 14:16: And He who sat on the cloud swung His sickle over the earth; and the earth was reaped.

There are two reapings of the harvest: In one God is harvesting His servants from the cities and kingdoms that are unworthy. There is another reaping in which God harvests all the sinners, leaving only the righteous. Thus He did in Noah and Lot's days. God will one day harvest His enemies because He wants to leave on earth an assembly of righteous people and Saints. Then God, tired of the wickedness of the ungodly who torment His servants, will deliver these from oppression.

Rev. 14:17–20: And another angel came out of the temple which is in heaven, and he also had a sharp sickle. And another angel, the one who has power over fire, came out from the altar; and he called with a loud voice to him who had the sharp sickle, saying, "Put in your sharp sickle, and gather the clusters from the vine of the earth, because her grapes are ripe." And the angel swung his sickle to the earth, and gathered the clusters from the vine of the earth, and threw them into the great wine press of the wrath of God. And the wine press was trodden outside the city, and blood came out from the wine press, up to the horses' bridles, for a distance of two hundred miles.

102

This gathering the clusters of the vine is the horrible vengeance of God against the enemies of those who love Him with a pure love. There will then be a strange slaughter lasting till the enemies of God are all defeated.

Those who shed Your blood and that of Your servants, who persecuted You in their sins, wanting to destroy and banish Your Spirit, those, oh Lord, will feel Your vengeance.

15

Rev. 15:1: And I saw another sign in heaven, great and marvelous, seven angels who had seven plagues, which are the last, because in them the wrath of God is finished.

When these seven last plagues have gone, there will not be any more suffering; the earth will be at peace and God's servants will be delivered from oppression.

If this is true for the cosmos, there is the same truth as it pertains to the individual . . . that is, the believer who is intended to reach the state of nothingness. This unproductive earth must suffer these seven plagues. After that there will be no more suffering for the planet . . . or for a formerly rebellious nature. There is no more cause for chastisement. Oh God, as long as there remains something of this living nature, Your wrath is so kindled against it that You do not let it have any rest. This refers to the souls God wants to bring to nought, destroy and then treat only with kindness. As long as they retain the least life, they meet only hardship.

Rev. 15:2: And I saw, as it were, a sea of glass mixed with fire, and those who had come off victorious from the beast and from his image and from the number of his name, standing on the sea of glass, holding harps of God.

There is a sea, perhaps in eternity, which is the Godhead. He is a sea in Whom the emptied believer is immersed and lost. But to reach this place, you – too – must be like a sea, that is . . . pure and transparent. The transparence and neatness of that sea is mingled with fire – with love. All saints, having been brought back to their origin and being one in God, are like small drops of water in this sea. They are not divided among themselves nor from the sea. All the blessed ones are in the divine unity of their principle. They are one with God though they are very distinct, just as the small drops have their own substance. These are the saints who will have been perfectly delivered and exempt from all self-interest.

The harps mentioned here are not their own; they are God's. This means they have lost all will of their own and received God's will in exchange. Be assured, such a believer has more freedom in the use of God's will than he ever had in using his own. Oh, the wonderful advantage the loss of all one's will affords! We receive no less than God's will! These harps have a constant harmony which God hears and which charms His heart and fills these poor souls with joy.

> **Rev. 15: 3,4: And they sang the song of Moses the bond-servant of God and the song of the Lamb, saying,**
> **"Great and marvelous are Thy works,**
> **O Lord God, the Almighty;**
> **Righteous and true are Thy ways,**
> **Thou King of the nations.**
> **Who will not fear, O Lord, and magnify Thy name?**
> **For Thou alone art holy;**
> **For all the nations will come and worship before Thee,**
> **For Thy righteous acts have been revealed."**

In this state, the soul of the believer can well sing the song with a wonderful harmony; God is doing the tuning within, having placed this one in the perfect order of His creation. He sings a twofold song, that of Moses which is a song of deliverance and that of the Lamb which is redemption's song. It is the more wonderful because those who sing it know how beneficial this redemption has been for them. Oh, if the mystery of redemption were well known (and the sacrifice of the Lamb), not a single Christian would be unwilling to die a thousand deaths.

Rack your brain by studying, get busy meditating as much as you please, you will not understand and know these great mysteries unless you count yourself as nothing.

An emptied soul receives such a pure knowledge of all that concerns God, of God Himself without study, with or without meditation; nothing is left to him. He gains with simplicity what others have learned so painfully. Ah, do not tire yourself studying as you do! Love, truly and purely, and you will learn more than in any other way.

But what is this song that these saints sing? If we are filled with all the words of it, we will easily notice the purity of their love, the eminence of their knowledge.

In the knowledge that is given them about the works of God, they say: Great and marvelous are Your works, oh Lord. The outward and inward works of God are uncovered and manifested to them with an unimaginable delight. They see everywhere, and in everything, the attributes of His power and the grandeur of God. By what they see they are overwhelmed with joy.

Oh God, how wonderful Your ways! However, men are so blind that they wish to measure God's ways by their thought. All which they do not clearly understand with their mind is, therefore, impossible to them!

Oh blindness and folly! Did not the apostle, admiring God's ways, say they were past finding out? His ways are "just and true," for all is just and true in God's conduct.

The whole earth will be converted to Jesus Christ and united to Him. All nations shall come and worship Him. Happy are those who will live then.

Rev. 15:5–8: After these things I looked, and the temple of the tabernacle of testimony in heaven was opened, and the seven angels who had the seven plagues came out of the temple, clothed in linen, clean and bright, and girded around their breasts with golden girdles. And one of the four living creatures gave to the seven angels seven golden bowls full of the wrath of God, who lives forever and ever. And the temple was filled wtih smoke from the glory of God and from His power; and no one was able to enter the temple until the seven plagues of the seven angels were finished.

106

The Scripture is so beautiful, so clear, that we are surprised people do not discover its beauty and clarity. There is a tabernacle of the testimony in each one of us. This temple is our spirit, where we receive the witness of the kindnesses of God, of His love for us and our love for Him. This tabernacle is within us like a sacred temple.

16

Rev. 16:1,2: And I heard a loud voice from the temple, saying to the seven angels, "Go and pour out the seven bowls of the wrath of God into the earth." And the first angel went and poured out his bowl into the earth; and it became a loathsome and malignant sore upon the men who had the mark of the beast and who worshiped his image.

What is said here refers to men in general, smitten with sin. However this very well describes what is happening to the souls in whom God wants to destroy carnality. God strikes them with a noisome and grievous sore, with all kinds of temptations.

Rev. 16:3: And the second angel poured out his bowl into the sea, and it became blood like that of a dead man; and every living thing in the sea died.

This person is overwhelmed with strange sufferings which leave him comfortless. This sea had been calm and peaceful for a long time. Every living soul died in the sea, which signifies that the fleshly and coarse feelings died.

Another meaning is that God hits the wicked with this second plague. The first chastisement was to punish sin with sin in this life. This second sin now is punished with stupefaction, numbness of the faculties, so that these people lose the brightness they had. They remain as useless as if they were dead, because their blood is as of a dead man; all seems snatched and quenched.

> **Rev. 16:4-6:** And the third angel poured out his bowl into the rivers and the springs of waters; and they became blood. And I heard the angel of the waters saying, "Righteous art Thou, who art and who wast, O Holy One, because Thou didst judge these things; for they poured out the blood of saints and prophets, and Thou hast given them blood to drink. They deserve it."

The third plague is fountains and rivers where the materially minded people took their pleasures.

These men, who so cruelly persecuted God's servants and had the best of their patience, made a boast of their wickedness and considered just the evil they had them endure, these will be punished in the same manner, sooner or later.

Your angels and saints rejoice because they consider these persecuted ones as their brothers. They love them so n .h more as they see in them the likeness of their Sovereign. You reserve for Yourself the day of vengeance, that day in which You will send all justice.

As for the soul God wants to strip, when He sends the third plague, He has His fountains, the sources of comfort. Yet, all that once cheered the soul changed into hardship and spoilage. There is not any more sweetness and peace; only suffering, distress, bitterness and grief. However, God is no less righteous.

> **Rev. 16:7:** And I heard the altar saying, "Yes, O Lord God, the Almighty, true and righteous are Thy judgments."

Oh men, you flatter yourselves, cover yourself with the mantle of an apparent piety, and you say you glorify God and work justly. "The judgments of God are true and righteous"; they will show that truth and righteousness are not in you.

> **Rev. 16:8,9:** And the fourth angel poured out his bowl upon the sun; and it was given to it to scorch men with fire. And men were scorched with fierce heat; and they blasphemed the name of God who

has the power over these plagues; and they did not repent, so as to give Him glory.

Here is the difference between the sinners and the righteous: the righteous accept their misfortunes and receive them with resignation. That resignation grows according to the trial the Lord gives them. Sinners get irritated and impatient against the evil and "blaspheme" dreadfully. These evils do not lead them inwardly. The sun which has only sweet influences in a temperate climate becomes scorching for these souls who burn with the fire of lust.

For the soul that God wants to strip, this fourth plague afflicts him very often with a strange burning within and without. This soul is tempted with blaspheming.

Some go through this in their spiritual life and do not understand. Instead of submitting and abandoning themselves to God, they do not wish to yield, and become furious when God is fighting in this soul to destroy their malignant nature. In his despair, this one may even set himself against God, when he should be going against his own self.

Rev. 16:10,11: And the fifth angel poured out his bowl upon the throne of the beast; and his kingdom became darkened; and they gnawed their tongues because of pain, and they blasphemed the God of heaven because of their pains and their sores; and they did not repent of their deeds.

The fifth plague afflicts one interested in goods and honor. This is the seat of the beast. One who had become fat with the possessions of the poor and weak ones becomes poor himself. This is the greatest grace God can send; however, sinners do not benefit by this grace and do not get converted; increasing their fury and blasphemy, "they repent not" of their evil deeds.

The seat of the beast, or her throne, is knocked down. Self-love and carnality are attacked in their source. This is the most cruel suffering this kind of soul could possibly know. This throne of self-love is full of darkness; there is no more light. These troubles, instead of sweetening man's nature and rendering it more pliable, cause violent anger; it may even look like demon possession. Poor nature! You may struggle but you must die. Defend yourself as much as you please; your resistance only increases and lengthens your torment.

> **Rev. 16:12-14:** **And the sixth angel poured out his bowl upon the great river, the Euphrates; and its water was dried up, that the way might be prepared for the kings from the east. And I saw coming out of the mouth of the dragon and out of the mouth of the beast and out of the mouth of the false prophet, three unclean spirits like frogs; for they are spirits of demons, performing signs, which go out to the kings of the whole world, to gather them together for the war of the great day of God, the Almighty.**

This plague, which seems so inferior to those which preceded it, surpasses them all; although the waters are changed into blood, they do not dry up completely. We must know that human nature is so eager for food that it prefers to feed and quench its thirst with trouble, than to be left without anything. The strong carnal souls feed themselves with the most terrible conditions.

As I am writing, a truth which I had never understood on being stripped is shown to me here. It is presented in this passage expressed clearly, telling us that some souls go through all the states which are intended to dispossess them and make them die out to their nature, yet they are not dispossessed, stripped nor dead to self. They remain alive in their circumstances; their very state becomes food for them. In the great light of eternity we will see souls which have gone through many states and they have become possessed of these very stages. We will never know this by what these persons say about themselves nor by our own judgment and reasoning power, but by the scent of the heart and by a supernatural light and insight that God gives.

Truly advanced souls embrace or reject things by the discernment of the heart. This discernment is fairer than any other. We do not discern these persons by what they say. A hundred miles away we may discern what is in the heart of a person. But human affectations must be entirely dead to have this discernment, otherwise our own inclination or dislike may become mixed into the matter.

When God does not want a thing (from these souls that are united to Him by an unbroken tie) He places them into suffering. This suffering eventually produces a kind of discernment. When such a person allows himself to be fully yielded to the leading of God, he possesses the least discernment of what God wants from him, or of what He wants from others, while others lack the poverty of their own spirit to yield to God.

We must notice that this can only and always be for a perfectly emptied soul which God designs to use for others. Let not people who live in the natural take this for themselves; however many are the states of grace they may have gone through, they will be deceived. Those who are in the first trials of hatred (or inclination to others) must not take this for themselves either, because then they are placed again in the natural plane, which God permits to purify them.

Returning to what I said, the natural man is so malicious that he prefers to be fed on evils, than to stay without food. He feeds even on hardest troubles; that is why the river was dried up, which is more troublesome to him than the change of the waters into blood. This river dries up to prepare the way of the kings. This passage is for the princes of this world. This dryness of the Euphrates refers to the dryness of all known graces (all props, even the most hidden ones), and all troubles whatever they may be. It is a total dryness of all that is and survives whether it be benefits, troubles, or even evils. This state is the hardest to fulfill.

It is also certain that there will be a terrible war and a gathering of kings who will fight against the victorious King who will uphold and defend the kingdom of our Lord.

The unclean spirits coming out of the mouth of the beasts which – again – are self-love, self-interest and carnality . . . or, in other words, those who are most opposed to pure love, are prideful ambition, love of independence, and covetousness. These three spirits stir the whole earth by fighting.

This is a general revolution, but the end will see all things subdued under the Kingdom of Jesus Christ. The fight will be dreadful, for Satan will defend himself with all his might.

Rev. 16:15: ("Behold, I am coming like a thief. Blessed is the one who stays awake and keeps his garments, lest he walk about naked and men see his shame.")

Oh God, You come as a thief, either when You overtake the sinner in his sin, or when You want to fill the soul with joy after trying her with so many evils.

Likewise when You come in Your wrath or to fill the world with joy at Your second advent, You will come as a thief when You are least expected.

But the watchful soul will be attentive; he will not be overtaken. (If she is taken by surprise, it will be with joy.)

We "keep our garments" by keeping the Spirit of Jesus Christ. He who keeps the Spirit of Jesus Christ, that is a spirit of self-denial and poverty, is well dressed, though he be deprived of all. But he who seems well dressed and is not inwardly stripped is naked, and his shame will appear even to those people who think that one is well dressed. The world interchanges the meaning of things. For them nakedness means one who is dispossessed; to be well dressed means wealth and carnality. However the carnal soul, appearing clothed, is in fact naked. That soul has not put on Jesus Christ; the poorest are well clothed; they have put on Jesus Christ.

Rev. 16:16: And they gathered them together to the place which in Hebrew is called Har-Magedon.

Here a battle must be fought among those who are kings. Some are kings because they reign by Jesus Christ, or rather, Jesus Christ reigns in and by them. They are truly kings because those who are perfectly submissive to God are made independent of the creation. This does not mean they will not obey their superiors, but that the creature is separated from them. They are seen as God sees, and obey as obeying God. Independence is not contrary to obedience for those who are supposed to obey; on the contrary obedience is more perfect than ever with them. But it does away with all subjection, all sight of the creature in what

113

is done, all power to act in view of pleasing when it is not God's will. These souls are free, unhindered by men.

These kings are gathered to fight other kings who are the princes of the world, who think they are kings. (They are slaves.) Those who are thought to be the most free in this world, are the most dependent and bound, and those who are believed to be bound are the most free. Those who are free with the freedom of Jesus Christ only know the weapons which are: trust in God, denial of all self, sacrificial spirit, and patience. The weapons of others are anger, passion, pride, arrogance, hatred, and reliance on their strength.

> **Rev. 16:17,18: And the seventh angel poured out his bowl upon the air; and a loud voice came out of the temple from the throne, saying, "It is done." And there were flashes of lightning, and sounds of peals of thunder; and there was a great earthquake, such as there had not been since man came to be upon the earth, so great an earthquake was it, and so mighty.**

This last blow is the stroke of grace which consumes all woes and which is the last of all misfortunes and the beginning of all blessings. The vial is poured out into the air, because it holds and pours out the entire capacity of the soul.

There came a great voice out of the temple. In other words the voice comes out of the depths of the soul. The voice seems to come from God Himself, saying: "It is done." These words designate that every hope is absolutely taken away from the soul. No resource is left. This is the most terrible and distressing state. It seems God confirms this. Human nature, seeing its last death blow, comes into frightful terrors, horrible alarms, and dreadful agitations, such as was not since men were on the earth. If this state is the greatest of all misfortunes, it is also the last.

When it pleases God to send His inner Spirit into the world, He does so only when it is about to be banished. When things are in a desperate condition, when truth is the most fought against, the most condemned, then will truth and light appear with the greatest brightness. But alas, before this, how many terrible thunderings and lightnings! It seems everyone will put on his armor to fight against truth if possible. Even those who are filled with truth go through terrors and strange frights, because of the evils threatening them. Things will be completely hopeless. "It is done" will be the word. But let us have patience. It is true there will be a consummation, but it will be the end of pains and the ruin of the enemies of truth.

This last persecution will be the strongest of all.

Rev. 16:19: And the great city was split into three parts, and the cities of the nations fell. And Babylon the great was remembered before God, to give her the cup of the wine of His fierce wrath.

It seems the soul is divided in three: There is a division of its superior and inferior part. The soul seems to think that within her are two promptings, one that is working and the other censuring the one that is working; one that is drawn to do something, the other condemning this move. One condemns, and the other, finding he is condemned, seeks the cause of the condemnation and finds it not. It seems that an army of reasoning powers are fighting each other, killing each other and continually coming back to life. This is a great torment.

In this battle in the soul, the cities of the nations – the refuges of human nature – are being lost and fall. In this struggle, it seems one pleads in behalf of the other, and has often the advantage, but finally is destroyed and defeated through a total sacrifice, and a perfect surrender. Human nature has no hope any more. In this fight, some self-will remains and would like to use its freedom to defend itself, like a drowning person using the little strength left to protect himself from death, but this effort causes him to die promptly.

The self comes in remembrance before God. This great Babylon, this mother of trouble and confusion, this enemy of peace, quietness, and simplicity, is remembered by God. But it is to give unto her the cup of the wine of the fierceness of His wrath.

Oh God, what a wine! It will be pure indeed. God will say to her: You did what I did not want; you rebelled against

Me. Now you will do what you don't want. Oh Babylon, by your confusion you trouble the earth! But you will be destroyed in a way that will astonish the earth.

Rev. 16:20: And every island fled away, and the mountains were not found.

All that which lifted up the soul and sustained it is destroyed. The soul does not find any more heights and depths. Once lifted up, she is now brought down. The soul has no greater stay than being sunk into the deepest humility.

Rev. 16:21: And huge hailstones, about one hundred pounds each, came down from heaven upon men; and men blasphemed God because of the plague of the hail, because its plague was extremely severe.

If God took away all props from the soul and did not have her feel the weight of His indignation, it would not be so bad. But bearing the weight of the wrath of God is most terrible. These thunderbolts constantly fall, fast and thick as hail. God adds all woes and withdraws any apparent stay and the soul is left helpless. With this comes persecution; no one remains to comfort.

Oh God, who could bear Your wrath?

When self is strong and carnality is big, human nature becomes so strangely furious that it would destroy itself if help was not sent. Some allow these blows to destroy them. Others resist violently and suffer so, that sometimes they die; or by repeated efforts, they leave their state, never to return again. That is, they lose their peace while the others, through these hardships, find an endless peace.

17

Rev. 17:1,2: And one of the seven angels who had the seven bowls came and spoke with me, saying, "Come here, I shall show you the judgment of the great harlot who sits on many waters, with whom the kings of the earth committed acts of immorality, and those who dwell on the earth were made drunk with the wine of her immorality."

Babylon, you must be condemned and destroyed. There is no more postponing. You are the one that sits on multitudes of sins as on "many waters"; you are resting on pleasures that are changing and flowing like the water. You are the great whore; you were created to be united to the will of God, and submitted to Him, You withdrew from your lawful Bridegroom to prostitute yourself to self, which used you to have iniquity with the whole world. You are living by sin, and feed on the wickednesses that cause your rebellion. You find your rest in the stir and the instability of waters; the torrents of iniquity have overflowed through you and your corruption has spread throughout the whole earth.

With you the kings of the earth have become corrupt, those who had been created to reign, for all men would have been kings if they had submitted to God. But because of you, wretched Babylon, the kings have become corrupt and slaves; and instead of tasting the everlasting delights for which they were created, delights that were pure and decent, you let them go astray, binding them to brutish and disgraceful pleasures by which they lose the delights of the Spirit. The whole earth is now full of this corruption and depravity. But you are condemned to die with the same drink you gave others. The wine you gave others to establish your kingdom, God will use to destroy you.

> **Rev. 17:3: And he carried me away in the Spirit into the wilderness; and I saw a woman sitting on a scarlet beast, full of blasphemous names, having seven heads and ten horns.**

Self-will is a woman, but an adulterous one, who has separated herself to prostitute herself; she who was intended to sanctify the earth, corrupted it. She dwells as in "the wilderness" because she cannot be adapted to any good. She sits on love of self which is scarlet colored because it mimics pure love. Isn't she manufacturing all sins, being the instrument of love of self?

Without her, there is no sin. These sins are red like scarlet because of their malice. She takes the liberty to commit all crimes because she wants everything which she likes. Although she is so wicked, and the source of all sin, at times she hides so well, that you cannot find her.

She is full of names of blasphemy because without ceasing she takes from God His attributes to ascribe them to herself. She is always rebellious and opposed to God. All I say about her wickedness is not even a semblance of what she is. Self-will is worse than all the devils. The sins on which she stands are not as evil as she is and the monster on which she sits has only the wickedness she imparts to him. Oh, self and wicked will!

If I could describe you, there is not a soul who would not hate you.

> **Rev. 17:4: And the woman was clothed in purple and scarlet, and adorned with gold and precious stones and pearls, having in her hand a gold cup full of abominations and of the unclean things of her immorality, ...**

This wretched will, in spite of her malevolence, has a dreadful shrewdness to hide herself and in this very thing she is most malignant. She hides herself with the appearance of all the virtues. She uses everything to reign. She is truly malignant. She holds "a gold cup ... full of abominations and of the unclean things of her immorality." The good cup does not prevent the malevolence of her poison. This malevolence is less strong and is in proportion to the self-will in the soul.

> **Rev. 17:5,6:** . . . and upon her forehead a name was written, a mystery, "Babylon the Great, the mother of harlots and of the abominations of the earth." And I saw the woman drunk with the blood of the saints, and with the blood of the witnesses of Jesus. And when I saw her, I wondered greatly.

This self-will is indeed a mystery that can hardly be discovered in most souls. She will even allow one to be quite severe in disciplining himself if only self is left in peace.

She feeds on everything, unconcerned and at her heart's content. She is not opposed to the outward practice of certain virtues; she survives and feeds on everything. What mystery! However, she is the mother of harlots because her actions (good in themselves when they come from God, their lawful Father) she transforms into bastards. She is the mother of abominations. God abominates all that comes from her. The martyrs have fought her. All the torments which God had them bear have only been to destroy her!

When there is no more self-will in the world, there will be no more sin.

> **Rev. 17:7,8:** And the angel said to me, "Why do you wonder? I shall tell you the mystery of the woman and of the beast that carries her, which has the seven heads and the ten horns. The beast that you saw was and is not, and is about to come up out of the abyss and to go to destruction. And those who dwell on the earth will wonder, whose name has not been written in the book of life from the foundation of the world, when they see the beast, that he was and is not and will come."

God must have this mystery be explained. As soon as this monster has been destroyed, sin will be completely destroyed. This beast ascends out of the bottomless pit, because sin rose from hell to earth through the serpent, but it rose to die pitifully, through the redemption of Jesus Christ Who destroyed sin, and re-established grace with more happiness than ever before. The lost ones and the devils shall wonder seeing this beast – self-love – is gone! They are lost because she is no more on earth. The lost will be desolate, and jealous of those who remain on earth. The Devil will have no power to tempt the faithful when self-will is banished from earth.

This self-will is rightly compared to Babylon on account of the trouble and confusion it brings in the soul. A will which is in concert with the will of God is like the ark which saves from the flood; it is the center of peace and rest.

How many souls there are who believe themselves to be without their own will, and are thought so by leaders, and in reality they are full of their own will! The self-will knows how to hide under the cover of an assumed obedience. When God places the soul in any condition pleasing to Him and it does not offer the least resistance, however terrible and amazing this condition may be, that soul stays abandoned to its God for all that He wills. In all the evils, he has no will or resistance. When the soul is not in a complete nothingness and loss, self may have some resistance though the will is submissive; but when self is really dead, there is no more resistance.

Often we are surprised that self resists more in the middle of the Christian life than in the start. In the beginning obedience is very easy. It seems we are in a perfect submission to all of God's will and to every trial. However, after a while, we feel the contrary. Self-will, at the beginning of the conversion, is still completely in the heart. Through conversion, its rebellion is taken away. On the other hand, in the sinner, self-will is entirely opposed to God's will. After conversion, though he has not this sinful rebellion, a Christian continues to have a thousand wishes that are opposed to God's. It is true he has not the will to rebel against God and to openly war against Him. After his conversion God has the soul entering a knowledge and a conscious love of His will. He does this with such kindness and gentleness that the senses and the outward life are sweetly drawn to do God's will. Strong desires of doing God's will come.

What, then, does self-will do? It goes deeper into the soul and does not appear at all outwardly, because self-will finds delights in the conscious desires of the will of God. This is not yet dangerous. Self-will hides, deep in the soul, feeding on delights; self-will is not fought against, and is at peace.

The soul, feeling this condition and finding no resistance within, thinks it has no will and does only God's will. The soul has no outward will, but has one inwardly, stronger than it ever was. When self-will leaves the outward life, it establishes itself within ... with more strength. The more the soul believes itself to be exempt from self-will, the more that soul has a deep, hidden will.

However, though it survives in all its strength, we assume there is no more rebellion. But what does God do? He Who has not given so many graces to a soul to allow this horrible monster to live within ... He will not allow this state to remain.

He takes all sweetness from the spiritual senses. He comes within this soul as an armed, strong man, to go after this will which is entrenched there. Then comes the suffering which has earlier been described. Self-will, which appeared dead and destroyed, is felt more than ever! Being hunted and chased its fury increases. The soul of the believer does not see God, but only his wicked will, getting worse every day. But the will becomes less dangerous the more it is uncovered. Self-will forsakes the deep, inner place of the believer and surfaces, appearing completely outward. Then she becomes rebellious again, as before conversion. Those who see these strange revolts and so little submission to God and His creatures are surprised, not understanding the mystery of self-will.

Finally, self-will is hunted so much that it has to depart!

The soul does not find any trace of it. The will of God is substituted and the soul has no will of her own any more. The soul is in possession of God's will, but only feels this when it resists God, or some of His wishes. She thinks this is self-will returned, again.

It is good, here, to warn the believer about some terrible dangers for the souls that are not entirely dead and brought to nothingness. One may think he is in such a state because he wishes to be so! Their will is very much alive, though hidden. It begins to appear, evidenced by this person's inclinations to follow his own desires, his nature, and thus strengthen his self-will. The self is not lost, but stronger. Thinking he follows the will of God, he follows his own and is drawn into strange sufferings which have no remedy, because he is persuaded he follows God's will.

There is another danger. Religious leaders adopt ideas on grace that suit the common rules ... their way to God is based on their dealings with those who have only the slightest desire to follow God. They know nothing when they meet a believer whose soul is perfectly brought to nought! The religious leader wants to oblige this one to go against his leadings (which are God's will for him). This ignorant religious leader places the Christian in a suffering which goes beyond all the torments which can be suffered on earth. When the religious leader finally sees that God works in him (or her), the leader esteems him less than a beginner!

Now a religious worker may say, "How can I know if this soul is one broken and one who has come to nothing ... or just a simple and pliable beginner? In one self is followed, in the other grace. Yet both have the same expressions."

Ah! How easy it is to know! You will see that the soul in nothingness is pliable in the hand of God in everything; he does not change his behavior in the face of the cross, which is the very opposite of others. He is always in the same submission. God has tried him though the cross and through blessings. A soul whom you see always supple and yielding for all God wants and is ready to agree always to His will, this soul must have experienced all deaths, all oppositions, all rebellions from the will, and is dead at last to every choice.

For others, on the contrary, they just come out of their pleasing and conscious state. They are full of themselves and can not long bear a cross. They do God's will only when it is their own, otherwise they openly resist His will.

Go, Christian worker – with all your might, against self-will; otherwise you will lose these believers without finding any remedy. You will see that your opposition to their self-will shall – in truth – hurt them ... but afterwards it will bring them peace.

Rev. 17:9,10: "Here is the mind which has wisdom. The seven heads are seven mountains on which the woman sits, and they are seven kings; five have

fallen, one is, the other has not yet come; and when he comes, he must remain a little while."

Self-will rests in the soul on seven mountains where it exercises its dominion. There are seven kings which desire thrones but the will is their sovereign. The seven mountains and the seven kings are ruled and captivated by her all at the same time. These seven mountains are intelligence, reason, judgment, discernment, wisdom, strength, and deliberation or choice. All appear to be the nobleness and the magnificence of the soul, the excellence of the mind. However, all these are subject to that will which rules them all. She leads them and directs everything. Jesus Christ said in His Gospel that if a blind man leads another, they both will fall in the ditch. The blind will also blinds the mind and drags it into her ditch with herself. She takes from man all his intelligence and eclipses his reason. She overthrows her judgment, darkens her discernment, destroys her wisdom.

Then, these become the "five kings that are fallen". One remains, which is strength. The power of deliberation and the power of choice represent the one who did not fall. His time has not arrived. He remains, the last of all.

When God wants to destroy self-will, He attacks the same things that self-will attacked when wanting to bring Him down from His throne. First He gives the light of intelligence, given with a great brightness and then extinguished. He gives keen judgment so as to condemn self-righteousness and to show that the will of God must be followed. But then He lets her lose this judgment. A clear discernment is given. Wisdom is given, but it appears to self-will as folly. At last self-will is dragged into blindness and the soul is reduced. The soul has no more choice left in it, and instinct seems to lead.

Rev. 17:11: "And the beast which was and is not, is himself also an eighth, and is one of the seven, and he goes to destruction."

The beast is the self-will in person. It was because it survived in these things and it is not as soon as these things are destroyed. It is the eighth because everything flows to him and he is the end of all these negative things. He is

123

numbered with the seven because he is in all these seven ones, and particularly in the choice or deliberation, for this is his main feature.

> **Rev. 17:12: "And the ten horns which you saw are ten kings, who have not yet received a kingdom, but they receive authority as kings with the beast for one hour."**

These ten horns are the ten passions which, joined with the beast, are eleven. This one is self-love, the beast. Till now, the revolt of passions had not yet come, but when they see the destruction of self-will and their own loss approaching, revolt comes. They all reside in the will, their seat. These passions appear for a little while only, with fury, and they will last as long as self-love is yet surviving. When self-will sees that will dying, he is like a lamp which, as it goes out, gives more light.

> **Rev. 17:13: "These have one purpose and they give their power and authority to the beast."**

Altogether they have only one mind. Self-love has all strength and power, so that it has all the ability to do what all the others cannot do among themselves.

> **Rev. 17:14: "These will wage war against the Lamb, and the Lamb will overcome them, because He is Lord of lords and King of kings, and those who are with Him are the called and chosen and faithful."**

Carnality with all his followers fights "against the Lamb" with all his strength, which means that the fight is against the Spirit of Jesus Christ, His reign and kingdom.

What is happening in the soul to establish the kingdom of Jesus Christ must happen in the whole Church to establish this kingdom!

After a strange fight and a terrible opposition from self-love, self-mind, self-will, and carnality against the Spirit of Jesus Christ, His reign and kingdom has the upper hand, finally. He overcomes and overrules the passions, changing them to His glory. Love will be changed to pure

124

love. Love will be the Captain and will devote to God all passions. Pure love will consecrate the enjoyment of even God which will be, for the soul, an untold delight. The desire will be all for God and His glory, the hatred for all that is opposed to God. Anger will be turned into zeal. Our Lord will overcome in this manner, and will use the same weapons that have been used against Him! He will confirm the soul in His love, giving it an unchangeable faithfulness.

> **Rev. 17:16: "And the ten horns which you saw, and the beast, these will hate the harlot and will make her desolate and naked, and will eat her flesh and will burn her up with fire."**

Jesus Christ uses the same weapons to fight that have been used to fight Him.

These shall hate the whore; hatred and anger rise against her, and make her desolate. As self-love ruled, self-will had the power and devoured all the good in the soul. Likewise as pure love rules, the will of God takes the place of self-will and devours it. At last it is burned in the fire of God's love.

Ah, wicked will, who will be able to understand all the evil that is in you! It goes beyond all that can be said about it. If you were not limited, we could say that you are as wicked as God is good. All I can say is that you are sovereign evil, the source and origin of all evils. I would prefer hell without you than heaven with you.

> **Rev. 17:17,18: "For God has put it in their hearts to execute His purpose by having a common purpose, and by giving their kingdom to the beast, until the words of God should be fulfilled. And the woman whom you saw is the great city, which reigns over the kings of the earth."**

God has put in their hearts these passions to do whatever He pleases to destroy and bring to nought this self-will. Then God gives up the passions for a while to an apparent confusion and disorder, and in this manner they destroy the self-will and strip from it all the garments it uses to cover itself. Then self-love seeing that the self-will is about to be destroyed and that if this happens, self-love will die too unless it finds some other pasture, this self-love takes all the power it has. What does it do? For self-preservation, it follows fast after the will, till at last the Word of God finds the time to fulfill all these things. When He comes, He destroys this self-love. Self-love purified by pure love is used of God as the rest.

This is the wonderful economy of the grace of redemption in Jesus Christ and it has cost Jesus Christ infinitely more than it costs the soul.

Self-will is the great Babylon reigning over the kings of the earth. It is fittingly compared to a great city, for it encloses noise, tumult, passions, sins and the commerce of people.

18

Rev. 18:1,2: After these things I saw another angel coming down from heaven, having great authority, and the earth was illumined with his glory. And he cried out with a mighty voice, saying, "Fallen, fallen is Babylon the great! And she has become a dwelling place of demons and a prison of every unclean spirit, and a prison of every unclean and hateful bird."

This powerful and shining angel that comes down from heaven is the will of God which descends into the soul as soon as self-will is banished. The will of God in God is God.

This "will" descends in the soul in proportion as the self-will is banished. It flows into the higher part of the soul first; just as self-will is chased from the higher to the inferior part of the soul. God's will takes the superior place, and always follows after this darker will, forcing it to move down.

What happens when it is fallen thus in the inferior part? It becomes the hold of every foul thing. Paul had felt this state when he said in Romans 7 that he felt in his members a law that resisted the law of his spirit. He had a will which wanted, and did, the right; and that was the will of God. He had another will that wanted, and did, evil; and that was this malignant will. The unclean birds are imagination and fantasies, and seem to dwell in them—so great are the thoughts and ridiculous imaginations at work.

We must notice that what happens in the individuals will happen in the Church. At the very end of self-will's reign, the children of the Church will be in a general corruption.

> Rev. 18:3: "For all the nations have drunk of the wine of the passion of her immorality, and the kings of the earth have committed acts of immorality with her, and the merchants of the earth have become rich by the wealth of her sensuality."

All men are born with a sense of carnality, with a rebellious will. It is a poison that has penetrated the substance of the soul, and that can be cured only by its antidote which is self-denial and the transformation of the will to that of God.

All men, being born free (and therefore kings), have committed fornication with her because there is no one that has not been seduced by this self-will which caused everyone to withdraw from the will of God. This woman draws into corruption man's sovereign freedom. Liberty, so beautiful and so noble – given only to do the will of God – has been corrupted so much by self-will that it seems, now, man uses this freedom only to oppose the will of God.

"The merchants of the earth" are the natural man unceasingly negotiating with the heart of man. They wax rich with their spoil, signifying that self-interest survives only through self-will and becomes rich with all that makes the soul poor (though it believes it makes it rich). The true wealth of pure love consists in having no will except God's.

> Rev. 18:4: And I heard another voice from heaven, saying, "Come out of her, my people, that you may not participate in her sins and that you may not receive of her plagues; ..."

If "Babylon" is the picture of self-will, it is also the picture of the corrupted nature. We are invited to come out of this Babylon, and that means to come out of ourselves. By this loss of self-will, the soul at last comes out of herself. We all are invited to this, we who want to be part of "the people of God" and of the inner and yielded souls; for the very mark of the people of God is to be inward and yielded.

Rev. 18:5,6: ". . . for her sins have piled up as high as heaven, and God has remembered her iniquities. Pay her back even as she has paid, and give back to her double according to her deeds; in the cup which she has mixed, mix twice as much for her."

God gets tired of the wickedness of this wretched and corrupted self-will; for her sins and her malices were not satisfied to stay in her low nature, but this malignant will reached unto heaven, signifying the superior part, or nature.

This is why God, so as to banish her from the soul entirely, begins to reward her as she deserves to be. And because she has been bold enough to attack God in the fulfillment of His will, God remembered all the iniquities of self-will. He gives power to the ministers of His justice to reward her as she deserves. She corrupted the entire human nature; but she must suffer all the penalty and drink in the same cup and in the same way what she has filled to men.

All the sins that she brought the soul into are used to punish and destroy her.

You wanted to rise to heaven: you will be thrust into depths of mud.

The punishment comes because of the insolence and rise of this self-will and because the soul fell into the deepest abyss of mud. If it were a pool of water, there would be some hope, but in a deep abyss of mud there is no hope of coming out. I am not surprised, oh prophet and king, that this deep abyss where you are plunged was the cause of your moanings.

Rev. 18:7,8: "To the degree that she glorified herself and lived sensuously, to the same degree give her torment and mourning; for she says in her heart, 'I sit as a queen and I am not a widow, and will never see mourning.' For this reason in one day her plagues will come, pestilence and mourning and famine, and she will be burned up with fire; for the Lord God who judges her is strong."

All the torments that God causes souls to suffer in the spiritual life are only in proportion to their pride.

The anger and despair we see are a pure effect of pride; so that all griefs have a mixture of it. God, to save the soul from sin, sent to its heart the fire of His love. And what did the malignant will do? It became allied with self-love. They fed, and became fat, on these divine tastes and used the kings in their prostitution.

What did this wretched Babylon say? I sit a queen on the throne, since I feed on spiritual possessions, and I will be obeyed as queen. I will be taken for the will of God. I am no widow. (That is why God strikes her, with plagues, afflictions and famine. Although it is said it all comes on one day, because of the promptitude and surprise this pounces on her, it does not end in a day. How happy she would be if it were so! This unfortunate Babylon is on a beast that has seven heads and in every one of these heads. When one of these heads seems wounded to death, it is found to live with more strength than before. She is burned and consumed by fire, so that nothing is left of her, not any trace or evidence. To that end has the Lord God Almighty condemned this wretched will.

> **Rev. 18:9: "And the kings of the earth, who committed acts of immorality and lived sensuously with her, will weep and lament over her when they see the smoke of her burning, ..."**

The kings of the earth represent the superior part of the soul and freedom, but that conspired, in weakness, with self-will. They bewail and lament with all their might. The burning is in the lower part, but the smoke rises to the superior part to stifle apparently the mind and surround it in this awful burning.

Oh God, this will also happen on the earth when this wretched will, which leads all men, shall be destroyed at last. But before its entire consummation, what griefs and pains!

> **Rev. 18:10: "... standing at a distance because of the fear of her torment, saying, 'Woe, woe, the great city, Babylon, the strong city! For in one hour your judgment has come.'"**

The more fire, death and ravage attack the inferior part

where the self-will has been rejected, the more the superior part of the soul remains aloof, stands afar off. The soul is not hunted; self-will is. But with fear it goes further away, saying: Alas! Alas! What a desolation! What a destruction!

> **Rev. 18:11–13:** "And the merchants of the earth weep and mourn over her, because no one buys their cargoes any more; cargoes of gold and silver and precious stones and pearls and fine linen and purple and silk and scarlet, and every kind of citron wood and every article of ivory and every article made from very costly wood and bronze and iron and marble, and cinnamon and spice and incense and perfume and frankincense and wine and olive oil and fine flour and wheat and cattle and sheep, and cargoes of horses and chariots and slaves and human lives."

The merchants of the earth are the outward and inward senses. They all mourn exceedingly, for their business or interchange is interrupted and all their pleasures lost. Two kinds of trades are spoken of, the outward senses dealing with earthly things only, and the inner senses having a more delicate work. When the ruin and destruction of the self comes, the inward and outward senses seem to think they will never have any pleasure again. But a finer taste will be given them by which they will be able to enjoy riches that are purely spiritual. This comes after the total destruction of this wretched Babylon.

> **Rev. 18:14,15:** "And the fruit you long for has gone from you, and all things that were luxurious and splendid have passed away from you and men will no longer find them. The merchants of these things, who became rich from her, will stand at a distance because of the fear of her torment, weeping and mourning, . . ."

To understand this passage, we must remember what has been said: Self, after having been chased into the lower part of the soul as her refuge, spreads out in this inferior part. At the start, she causes the senses to be pleased and she is received as a hostess. Then these merchants witness her griefs, and stand afar off departing from her. Self-will remains deadened and the soul lives in the will of God.

> **Rev. 18:16,17: "... saying, 'Woe, woe, the great city, she who was clothed in fine linen and purple and scarlet, and adorned with gold and precious stones and pearls; for in one hour such great wealth has been laid waste!' And every shipmaster and every passenger and sailor, and as many as make their living by the sea, stood at a distance, ..."**

What a wonderful description of the self-will. See her in triumph and see her in the state to which she is reduced when she is destroyed! Nothing is as big as the will of man, leading and governing everything. Everything bends under her, and obeys her. She is "clothed" and decorated with all the finest things there are; "the purple and scarlet" belonging to love are her main ornaments. With this queen of all virtues, everything is given her, as long as she is in the order of the will of God. She is then in untold delights. But as soon as this will, which is so fine, looks upon herself as such, she gets a sense of carnality concerning her blessing and at the same time becomes haughty and rebellious. She misuses these riches and draws to her man's freedom and they, together, become polluted. Self-will wishes to rob God of everything. Instead of the love to which she was united and by which she was surrounded with goodness, loaded with riches, she unites with self-love which, with self-interest, gets into strange usurpations. Then she prostitutes herself to self-love and to self-interest. God bears with her for a while with much patience, but at last His anger is stirred against her, and then it is that her magnificence is changed into disgrace. All those who noticed this change depart from this wretch. (These are all the faculties of the soul and senses.)

> **Rev. 18:18,19: "... and were crying out as they saw the smoke of her burning, saying, 'What city is like the great city?' And they threw dust on their heads and were crying out, weeping and mourning, say-**

ing, 'Woe, woe, the great city, for in one hour she
has been laid waste!' "

Self-will is very fittingly compared to a "great city,"
because the will encloses all the operations of the soul.

However this haughty and wicked city is made desolate
in an hour. That is, in the time planned by God for its ruin.

It is certain that the smoke of her burning rises high.
Everyone who has known these people, and the soul, are
surprised at such destruction. They cannot understand
how such opposed states come in so little time. Nevertheless the measure of the evils is the measure of the blessings.

**Rev. 18:20: "Rejoice over her, O heaven, and you
saints and apostles and prophets, because God has
pronounced judgment for you against her."**

Nothing in the world is as beautiful as, "Rejoice over
her, O heaven."

Oh Church, rejoice over her, because all the troubles of
your children for whom you sigh are going to be banished
from your midst, since the one who is the source of them
is destroyed.

And you, holy apostles and prophets in the Church,
rejoice because the fruit of your work is going to be fulfilled
through the ruin of this wretched will.

When self-will is destroyed, the soul is judged forever
and can enjoy her God. Oh souls, rejoice in your deepest
misfortunes and the evils you must suffer for the destruction of self-will, for this judgment is enclosed in her condemnation. If it is not condemned and destroyed, you are
condemned to sufferings in this life and the next; but if she
is condemned and destroyed, there is only salvation, joy
and peace for you.

**Rev. 18:21: And a strong angel took up a stone like
a great millstone and threw it into the sea, saying,
"Thus will Babylon, the great city, be thrown down
with violence, and will not be found any longer."**

This mighty angel is the will of God which has condemned self-will as his main enemy. Self-will is cast in the sea like a stone, so that it is never more found.

Hell is the abyss into which carnality is plunged, to come out no more. But the bosom of God is the wonderful abyss where the good will is lost and sunk never more to be found, for there it is changed into the will of God.

Rev. 18:22,23: "And the sound of harpists and musicians and flute-players and trumpeters will not be heard in you any longer; and no craftsman of any craft will be found in you any longer; and the sound of a mill will not be heard in you any longer; and the light of a lamp will not shine in you any longer; and the voice of the bridegroom and bride will not be heard in you any longer; for your merchants were the great men of the earth, because all the nations were deceived by your sorcery."

Here two kinds of things are spoken of, which feed self-will; first, the conscious delights of the mind, and the delight of this wretched selfish soul with outward self-denials which increase her pride and the delights of her mind.

There is such a combination between the devil, the corrupted nature, self-will, and self-interest that they work together in accord. But since self-will has a great power, after the dragon yielded all his power to self-love, and that self-love yielded his to self-will, the devil, in order to increase self-will, transfigures himself into an angel of light and sends her illustrations which are considered to be very great graces. As often happens, God, to withdraw the soul from the most dangerous effects of this will and of sin, caresses this soul and has her hear His sweet voice which is the voice of the Bridegroom to the soul. Carnality plunges forever into the pit where it finds greater torments than ever she had pleasures and corruptions on earth.

This is also what will happen to the Church and the world at large, just as it happens to an individual's soul which God wants to strip. Then men will be holy because they will all walk in the will of God. This state shall continue as long as this wretched carnality, or self-greed, remains chained in the pit. But, oh God, as soon as the chains are broken and that new power to hurt men is given to her, with what fury she will use it for revenge!

Rev. 18:24: "And in her was found the blood of prophets and of saints and of all who have been slain on the earth."

While this wretched carnality is in the soul, we do not know the damages she causes; on the contrary men believe that all the evils and sufferings come on them because they are not faithful enough to worldliness! Nevertheless, the more we try to be faithful to carnality, the more she increases her tyranny. They think she will ease the pains which they do not know come by her, till her judgment appears. As soon as she is condemned and destroyed, it is known that in her was found the blood of prophets and of saints, because they discover that it was she who caused all the inner sufferings as well as the outward ones. She was the reason that all lights had been put out and that holiness was, as it were, banished from the soul. But she has so much malice that this can be found out only after her destruction. On the contrary she makes the soul think she is the source of all blessings, when actually it is certain that she alone is the cause of all the evils that happen, not only to the individual soul, but to all the earth, generally speaking.

19

Rev. 19:1,2: After these things I heard, as it were, a loud voice of a great multitude in heaven, saying, "Hallelujah! Salvation and glory and power belong to our God; because His judgments are true and righteous; for He has judged the great harlot who was corrupting the earth with her immorality and He has avenged the blood of His bond-servants on her."

Heaven will rejoice when carnality is banished from earth because it will then be the time of the glory and reign of God on earth, since His will shall be done on earth as in heaven. This is the joy of the saints in heaven and of those on earth, when they see this evil condemned.

The other heaven, the inner one in the depth and center of the soul, rejoices after the destruction of this will which is so carnal. Then the soul knows the great advantages that have come to her by the destruction of this self-will, and how righteous it was that she would suffer all she did. In the depth of her joy and delight she cannot help praising her God, and giving Him endless thanks for His wonderful works.

Rev. 19:3,4: And a second time they said, "Hallelujah! Her smoke rises up forever and ever." And the twenty-four elders and the four living creatures fell down and worshiped God who sits on the throne saying, "Amen. Hallelujah!"

Again they said: Alleluia, for we cannot praise God enough for such a great benefit. The work of the whole life will be praising God and admiring His mercies after such a deliverance. Truly God uses painful means to destroy self-will.

Then all the saints, all that is great and holy in the soul, praise and adore Him. How do they? By their nothingness, shown by their falling down prostrated.

Rev. 19:5: And a voice came from the throne, saying, "Give praise to our God, all you His bond-servants, you who fear Him, the small and great."

Oh God, your servants will be busy praising You throughout eternity — and this must be their occupation in time.

Three kinds of praises are mentioned here and they are all according to the will of God.

This revelation of Jesus Christ is one of the most sublime states in this life.

The soul in whom Jesus Christ has revealed Himself offers to God the most sublime praises in this life. It is a praise of sacrifice. This is the greatest praise God can draw from His creatures. This is the mystery of Christian religion and of the most perfect state in it. But these deep truths, these forms of worship so worthy of God, are ignored by men. Oh truths, when you are manifested, all this will be uncovered.

Rev. 19:6,7: And I heard, as it were, the voice of a great multitude and as the sound of many waters and as the sound of mighty peals of thunder, saying, "Hallelujah! For the Lord our God, the Almighty, reigns. Let us rejoice and be glad and give the glory to Him, for the marriage of the Lamb has come and His bride has made herself ready."

All saints in Heaven, angels and men will rejoice when this vile Babylon is destroyed and taken from earth. This reign could take place only when the will of God was fulfilled on earth as in heaven.

But notice the wonderful expression in the Scripture. It does not say we must rejoice because He is made king since He was born king, as He told Pilate. But the Scripture says we must praise God because the Lord God omnipotent reigns. He was king, but did not enjoy the complete possession of His reign.

But what must delight us is the fact that the marriage of the Lamb is come. Oh, holy and spotless Church, you are the Bride of the Holy Spirit; but up to now, there has been no marriage. The Lamb came to be the Spouse of all the souls. That was His dearest desire. He expressed it before dying: "Father, may they be one as we are one." However, this church, though one in faith, is filled with rebellious members with a rebellious will, preventing this marriage. It is one in spirit because those who withdraw cease to be her children. But she is not one in love. However all will have to become one so that Jesus Christ will reign everywhere. This will be the greatest joy in Heaven and the greatest happiness on earth. Oh happy day, the day of triumph for the Lamb!

The Bride will be prepared through the loss and stripping of all that was opposed to her Bridegroom. She invites herself and everyone to rejoice because she discovers now what it means for God to enter His reign within. There is no resistance; it is a complete submission.

Rev. 19:8: And it was given to her to clothe herself in fine linen, bright and clean; for the fine linen is the righteous acts of the saints.

With this marriage, the Bride is clothed with the robe of innocence. Jesus Christ wants to give all men this robe of innocence and purity, and after centuries of abomination will follow those of innocence and simplicity, a natural state, all revealing Jesus Christ Who will extend the power of His redemption given by His Father for men. This robe given to the Church will be the righteousness of the saints. They will be godly; they will be placed in the Truth. This is what will take place at the marriage of the Lamb.

This spotless Lamb arrays her with the robe of innocence, simplicity, which is the brightest that ever was. This is abundant redemption in Christ.

Rev. 19:9: And he said to me, "Write, 'Blessed are those who are invited to the marriage supper of the Lamb.'" And he said to me, "These are true words of God."

This supper is simply the sacrifice, or mystic death, which souls are called to go through. No one is admitted unless he has been invited, called, sacrificed, dead, brought to nought. Oh blessed supper, where the Lamb Himself feeds the souls that He wants for His Bride.

Rev. 19:10: And I fell at his feet to worship him. And he said to me, "Do not do that; I am a fellow servant of yours and your brethren who hold the testimony of Jesus; worship God. For the testimony of Jesus is the spirit of prophecy."

The angel teaches us that we must not stop at the least thing, however excellent it may appear, because it is not above us but on our level. Oh men, you do not understand your dignity and nobility, otherwise you would not stop at a thousand things that are unworthy of what you are.

The angel certifies that those who have within the testimony of Jesus are equal to him, an angel, no less! In the highest form of worship, we must pass by everything, and stop only with Him!

Rev. 19:11,12: And I saw heaven opened; and behold, a white horse, and He who sat upon it is called Faithful and True; and in righteousness He judges and wages war. And His eyes are a flame of fire, and upon His head are many diadems; and He has a name written upon Him which no one knows except Himself.

The second advent of Jesus Christ is not the last judgment but the day of His manifestation. This manifestation will take place throughout the earth, and in His whole Church, as it is in the individual soul.

He is the Faithful and the True One. Anything else is a lie. He sits on a white horse. Innocence and righteousness He imparts to the soul.

His eyes are as flames of fire, to indicate His perfect love burning within. He is crowned with many crowns because apart from the crown due Him by His birth, He acquired many by the victories He won. His name is known of Himself alone. This name is the strength and power that God gave Him.

Rev. 19:13: And He is clothed with a robe dipped in blood; and His name is called The Word of God.

The Word of God, through Jesus Christ, had a vesture dipped in blood. The humanity of Christ was like the vesture of Divinity. Through His death Jesus Christ conquered; truth triumphed destroying the lie that had held it captive.

Jesus Christ must then reign throughout the whole earth, for He will reign over the hearts as well as over the minds of men.

Rev. 19:14,15: And the armies which are in heaven, clothed in fine linen, white and clean, were following Him on white horses. And from His mouth comes a sharp sword, so that with it He may smite the nations; and He will rule them with a rod of iron; and He treads the wine press of the fierce wrath of God, the Almighty.

All of heaven is being armed to destroy the lie and to establish the truth. All are on white horses as their Captain; this shows innocence, righteousness, justice. These uphold truth. They are clothed in fine linen white and clean, which shows they are upheld in righteousness and innocence, their clothing.

There goes out of the mouth of Jesus Christ a sharp sword with two edges. That is simply His Word manifesting the truth. He then comes with this weapon to smite all that is opposed to the truth. He will rule uprightly. Oh God, till now Your reign has been divided in the hearts and on the earth. But time is at hand when You will reign alone on earth and in the hearts, and no one will share Your authority.

Rev. 19:16: And on His robe and on His thigh He has a name written, "King of kings, and Lord of lords."

The name of Jesus Christ bears the power that was given to Him when He became a man and shows how God gave Him royalty and power. The name written on His thigh, meaning His power as a man that was given Him. He must be King of kings; all the earthly kings must be subject to Him, not only outwardly, by receiving faith, but inwardly, by receiving His Spirit. Then will Jesus Christ reign making all men kings. He will be King of kings and Lord of lords because He will meet no resistance.

Rev. 19:17,18: And I saw an angel standing in the sun; and he cried out with a loud voice, saying to all the birds which fly in midheaven, "Come, assemble for the great supper of God; in order that you may eat the flesh of kings and the flesh of commanders and the flesh of mighty men and the flesh of horses and of those who sit on them and the flesh of all men, both free men and slaves, and small and great."

This angel which is in the sun is the herald of the truth. He will invite all men to come and admire its light. But before this, oh God, what a horrible fight must be fought on earth! Oh God, nothing will be able to come against You on the earth or in the heart of man. He is a conqueror Who wants to possess His conquests. He ransacks all that opposes His kingdom. Oh Princes, open your gates and the King of glory shall come in! Oh men, open your hearts and your minds and receive within this King of glory Who comes to stay!

Rev. 19:19: And I saw the beast and the kings of the earth and their armies, assembled to make war against Him who sat upon the horse, and against His army.

The beast is self-love, a follower of the lie, the one who

has seduced all men and made them to be contrary to love and truth, for truth and love cannot be separated. This self-love gathers all his followers to make war with all their might against pure love. They see they are about to be ruined and then they do the most damage and are armed with more might.

This is true for both the individual and the world at large. Self-love has never put up so much effort than at the time of his destruction; the lie has never seemed stronger than when he is about to vanish away to be replaced by truth. But their efforts are useless. The kings are powerless, the mighty are without strength; nothing will be able to resist this Sovereign King. They war against Jesus Christ and do not know it. He knows how to revenge and defend His cause.

Rev. 19:20,21: And the beast was seized and with him the false prophet who performed the signs in his presence, by which he deceived those who had received the mark of the beast and those who worshiped his image; these two were thrown alive into the lake of fire which burns with brimstone. And the rest were killed with the sword which came from the mouth of Him who sat upon the horse, and all the birds were filled with their flesh.

The beast is taken and with him the false prophet, that is the lie, who by his deception and apparent miracles has deceived all men, preventing them from siding with the truth, making them choose self-love instead of pure love. But now when Jesus Christ comes and appears in His reign, this monster must be taken. But as soon as Jesus Christ appears, the beast and the prophet must be taken by Jesus Christ Who is love and truth. Oh Jesus, as soon as You come, this hellish monster, this wretched self-love, does not resist You any more! Self-love and "Lie" came out of hell, just as the truth came from God. Jesus Christ then came to have them return to their own place and to bring truth on earth. Henceforth the reign of Jesus Christ is the reign of truth and pure love, as the reign of the devil had been the reign of self-love and lies.

Oh God, now indeed is the reign of self-love and the lie. Come, Lord Jesus, to destroy them.

20

Rev. 20:1-3: And I saw an angel coming down from heaven, having the key of the abyss and a great chain in his hand. And he laid hold of the dragon, the serpent of old, who is the devil and Satan, and bound him for a thousand years, and threw him into the abyss, and shut it and sealed it over him, so that he should not deceive the nations any longer, until the thousand years were completed; after these things he must be released for a short time.

This angel coming down from heaven shows the whole power of God. He has the key of the bottomless pit. This power was given to Jesus Christ and He has the same right to shut the pit as He had to open heaven. Till now, though this redemption is for all, it has not been extended effectively to all men. The failure is not on the part of the Redeemer, but it is the fault of the wicked will of man opposing the effectiveness of redemption. Jesus Christ, seeing that it was impossible for the covetous man to enter heaven, and that so long as self-will would stay on earth, it would corrupt some continuously, He first destroyed this covetousness wherever it was established, in every man. Apparently it is only one monster, however it is composed of an infinity of monsters. When He has destroyed it and sent it to the pit from which it came, what else does Jesus Christ do? Since the devil would bring it back, God casts him into the bottomless pit, which he seals and for a thousand years he will not be able to hurt men.

Now the devil has not any power on the souls that are free from covetousness. God, however, at the end of their lives allows them to be tempted outwardly. Then come the hardest knocks, but the temptations remain without any effect, because God Himself protects them, shortening the time of temptation to a little season. God's way, here, is wonderful. To how many evils does He not deliver the soul in order to free her from covetousness? But it is certain that when it is freed, the devil is bound.

Rev. 20:4: And I saw thrones, and they sat upon them, and judgment was given to them. And I saw the souls of those who had been beheaded because of the testimony of Jesus and because of the word of God, and those who had not worshiped the beast or his image, and had not received the mark upon their forehead and upon their hand; and they came to life and reigned with Christ for a thousand years.

The judgment was given to those who leave all to follow Jesus Christ. The grace of judging everything is given to those who gave up all these things. They will judge others through the discernment that will be given them. When it is spoken of the souls that were beheaded, those are meant who have been deprived of the natural use of their powers, who allowed themselves to be completely stripped of them, in order to witness for Jesus Christ, letting Him reign in them and being subject to Him. The soul reigns and lives because she lives with the life of Jesus Christ. Till this life comes into the soul, all other lives are deaths. The only life that can bear the name of life is imparted by a mystic resurrection.

Rev. 20:5,6: The rest of the dead did not come to life until the thousand years were completed. This is the first resurrection. Blessed and holy is the one who has a part in the first resurrection; over these the second death has no power, but they will be priests of God and of Christ and will reign with Him for a thousand years.

The other dead are those who during this life have a

mystic death; these will enter a new life. How fortunate they are! "This is the first resurrection," the mystic resurrection of which much has been said. These are truly happy for several reasons. First, sin has no more power over them. Then, natural death does not trouble them; it is only a gentle sleep for them and no death. How truly blessed and holy is he who has entered the true resurrection! They are priests of God and of Jesus Christ for they are kept for the greatest sacrifices and to sacrifice themselves constantly. They shall reign with Him a thousand years. The thousand years cannot be understood literally, by the letter of the word; rather it is a time that God alone knows, in which the individual soul and also the whole earth are to be placed in a consistent state to reign with Jesus Christ.

The reign and blessedness of the creature is depending on that of Jesus Christ. Oh, wonderful reign which is going to extend on earth; you will but be the sample of the reign Jesus Christ must have in eternity.

> **Rev. 20:7-9: And when the thousand years are completed, Satan will be released from his prison, and will come out to deceive the nations which are in the four corners of the earth, Gog and Magog, to gather them together for the war; the number of them is like the sand of the seashore. And they came up on the broad plain of the earth and surrounded the camp of the saints and the beloved city, ...**

Whatever will happen in the Church in the end is happening in the soul.

After the soul has remained a long time in a state of steadfastness, when Jesus Christ is reigning within and the soul rules over the devils that have no power over it, then for a while the devil is released for God's glory and for the finished work in the soul. In no time it seems he stirs everybody and even sets the soul against its own self. Oh God, he leaves no stone unturned. He sets against the soul cities and kingdoms. But all his efforts are useless. God never protected her better though He seems to deliver her to her foes entirely. This attack is different from the first ones, in this way: In the first, the soul defended itself against its foes; then its weakness was such that the soul surrendered. But here it is attacked by all hell and does not defend itself; nor is the soul weak. God is its strength and defense.

> Rev. 20:9b–10: . . . and fire came down from heaven and devoured them. And the devil who deceived them was thrown into the lake of fire and brimstone, where the beast and the false prophet are also; and they will be tormented day and night forever and ever.

God destroys this deadly foe of mankind in a moment. He seems to be set free so as to be condemned forever. The torment he will bring on the saints will be short and will serve to establish them forever in eternal rest.

> Rev. 20:11: And I saw a great white throne and Him who sat upon it, from whose presence earth and heaven fled away, and no place was found for them.

Here is a wonderful illustration of nothingness. Before God comes in all His majesty, heaven and earth appear. As soon as He clothes the soul with the state of innocence, He sits "on the great white throne," which He prepared for Himself to rest there eternally. The whole soul, earth, heaven, must be lost in God. Then God remains alone. The soul is not divided any more. She knows nothing, only God; and God remains in all His glory and majesty.

> Rev. 20:12,13: And I saw the dead, the great and the small, standing before the throne, and books were opened; and another book was opened, which is the book of life; and the dead were judged from the things which were written in the books, according to their deeds. And the sea gave up the dead which were in it, and death and Hades gave up the dead which were in them; and they were judged, every one of them according to their deeds.

This is the last judgment. Those who died with a mystic death will no longer be able to fear hell or sin. Those who are truly dead will be received in God. All will be judged according to their works, and works are no good unless they are done in the will of God.

> **Rev. 20:14,15: And death and Hades were thrown into the lake of fire. This is the second death, the lake of fire. And if anyone's name was not found written in the book of life, he was thrown into the lake of fire.**

Death and hell are over and there is no more death for the soul. All is life and freedom. But he who did not go through the first death, must suffer the second death. This is for those who are dead in sin. This refers to those who have not a new life in Jesus Christ. He is "the book" in which all the predestined ones are written.

If we read carefully this book of "Revelation," we would see that all the possible states of the divine and spiritual life are contained there.Lre. And if anyone's name was not found written in the book of life, he was thrown into the lake of fire.

21

Rev. 21:1: And I saw a new heaven and a new earth; for the first heaven and the first earth passed away, and there is no longer any sea.

The soul has gone through all the states which have been described. Heaven and earth now vanish away. Physical and spiritual principles now join here. What is earthy and material in creation, and in the believer, is destroyed! As soon as He comes in His majesty, all must disappear and make room for Him. This is the mark of His greatness and might. As we see mountains of snow melt and crumble before the sun, so when the majesty of God appears, the entire soul must vanish away and disappear. All that is not entirely destroyed may remain by some grace, but whatever it is, it is not God Himself! Oh God, as soon as You appear, any life, any subsistence in creation, in the believer, in me vanishes away! Only nothingness is left, giving You room to be all!

Oh wonderful result! The wonderful and divine union of the Bridegroom and Bride takes place. It is not only a close union, but all is reduced to the unity of their principle. There the Bride becomes one with her Bridegroom. There is no more distinction between them. There, having no self-existence, she is in God. This is the perfection of all happiness; there is worked out and perfected a perfect nothingness. There, she is made one with God, and is really so lost in Him that she cannot be separated any more from Him.

Two different states are wonderfully described in this book of Revelation. The first state is explained by "the heaven when it is rolled like a scroll" (Rev. 6:14). This is the soul losing her quality to take that given by God. But this heaven that was rolled kept its place. The second state is marked by "the passing away of heaven and earth"; it is not only rolled but it vanished away, disappearing before the majesty of God.

After the soul is lost, sunk, united with God, she loses all. He gives her Jesus Christ Who becomes her new heaven and her new earth. Everything is given back to her with an unthought-of advantage. She can then do anything without coming out of her unity. She has become "a new creature" in Jesus Christ. Everything is given her in Jesus Christ; and Jesus Christ is all in her. This old creature is no more spoken of; she is completely made new, and nothing remains of the old.

As for "the sea" that is no more, this means that the storms and tempests are no longer.

Rev. 21:2: And I saw the holy city, new Jerusalem, coming down out of heaven from God, made ready as a bride adorned for her husband.

John speaks here very clearly of the renewal which must take place in the Church. The Spirit of the Church will be renewed on the whole earth. This is this Spirit of the Word possessing her; however it is quite far from its members. This Spirit then will spread everywhere, renew the whole earth, according to the promise given. Then "the new Jerusalem will come down from heaven."

Referring to the individual soul, it means that the works of the soul, within or without, "come from heaven." It is a state of glory and triumph given to her; it is given her to do on earth what is being done in heaven. After her renewal, all within her does not proceed from her since "she is no more," but all is from God and this is the strength and effectiveness of her works. She then comes "prepared and adorned." God gives the Church, outwardly, all the excellence and splendor that the majesty of God (and the grace that she shares) deserve.

Rev. 21:3: And I heard a loud voice from the throne, saying, "Behold, the tabernacle of God is among men, and He shall dwell among them, and

they shall be His people, and God Himself shall be among them, . . ."

The soul, yea, and the Church – having reached this place through such rough and strange ways and being so perfectly transformed – is now the tabernacle of God where He dwells and rests with unspeakable delight.

This refers both to the renewed Church and the soul, which will be the tabernacle of God. Then will God delight to dwell with men, and He will truly be their God, and they shall be His people. Then this nothingness which molds a soul in God and makes her one with Him, will also mold them and perfect their unity in God.

Rev. 21:4: ". . . and He shall wipe away every tear from their eyes; and there shall no longer be any death; there shall no longer be any mourning, or crying, or pain; the first things have passed away."

There are no more sorrows, tears, or afflictions because there is no more death; no more nothingness to complete. When nothingness is not completely perfected, there may be always suffering here on earth. But here in this scene all these things have gone except peace, joy, and satisfaction.

This will be the time of triumph both for the Church and Jesus Christ. After having exhibited a suffering Christ for so long, the Church now will exhibit Him glorious and triumphant.

Rev. 21:5: And He who sits on the throne said, "Behold, I am making all things new." And He said, "Write, for these words are faithful and true."

How true it is, oh God, that You are going to make "all things new." The souls, Your spouses, and Your Church! Oh, new state, new life, new everything, all will be made new! There is not one soul who would not experience this if she surrendered herself fully to God.

Rev. 21:6: And He said to me, "It is done. I am the Alpha and the Omega, the beginning and the end. I will give to the one who thirsts from the spring of the water of life without cost."

150

After all these states are passed away, all is done, and the soul is in a perfect consummation because Jesus Christ is the beginning and the end. By Him all the states start — and end — by Him. The soul begins by Jesus Christ, and by Him all is finished and consummate.

All begins by the love of Jesus Christ. We surrender to Him; He leads, being the way, by paths that are closed to all but Him. And when He leads the believer through horrible and frightful deserts, He leads him to the end. As long as "the way" lasts the soul does not notice that Jesus Christ leads him. He hides to have him lose all distinction of his own; and bring him in unity. When he reaches this place, then He appears as the truth and He places him in the truth of God. The soul discovers the whole of God and the nothingness of the creature. In this truth, it seems to him that all, up to now, was error, lie, deceit, blindness.

But when the believer is in this truth of his perfect unity with God, suddenly Jesus Christ is given him as life. After having borne all these states in his soul, after having sacrificed himself, He is glorified in him and He glorifies him, having him enter His glory and joy. And through all eternity He will be glorified in this soul, so that, after having been crucified and sacrificed, we will be glorified as His!

That was what Jesus Christ said to His disciples. "My Father is in me; you are in Me and I am in you." And again: "My Father, glorify Me now with Your own self, with the glory I had before the world was." "All I have is Yours; all You have is Mine. I am glorified in them." This is the state of Jesus Christ glorified in the soul. This is the perfection of all men in Jesus Christ; when they are all united in the unity of essence where God, in His Word, is all, and works out all Himself without Whom nothing was ever created.

"I in them and Thou in Me that they may be made one." The Father flows through the Word, into the soul, and the soul is brought back to God by being lost in God.

After saying He is "the principle and the end," Jesus Christ says He "will give to the one who thirsts from the spring of the water of life without cost." How deceived are those who wait for means to buy this water! Jesus Christ gives it freely; we have only to go to Him, to ask for it. After showing that the perfection of the soul begins and ends in Him, He shows how easy it is to enter in. It could be said that these states are not for everybody, that it is difficult to enter in. Jesus Christ assures that He will give of the fountain of the water of life to all those that are athirst. We will not believe a special merit is needed to have this water! And you may come boldly, knowing you have no means to repay.

Rev. 21:7: "He who overcomes shall inherit these things, and I will be his God and he will be My son."

The victory that Jesus Christ requires of us is not a victory that we must win ourselves. We are so weak that we would be defeated, and not overcomers. God with His Word fought for them and won the victory. But what does this victory consist in? Those in whom He won these victories are truly His sons.

Rev. 21:8: "But for the cowardly and unbelieving and abominable and murderers and immoral persons and sorcerers and idolaters and all liars, their part will be in the lake that burns with fire and brimstone, which is the second death."

All those who are in these vices will not enter this inner kingdom without leaving their vices.

The fearful ones are always stopped by fear; they never abandon themselves to God. The unbelievers lack a great faith to believe, without any motive to do so!

Rev. 21:9,10: And one of the seven angels who had the seven bowls full of the seven last plagues, came and spoke with me, saying, "Come here, I shall show you the bride, the wife of the Lamb." And he carried me away in the Spirit to a great and high mountain, and showed me the holy city, Jerusalem, coming down out of heaven from God ...

This bride, the Lamb's wife, is the glorified Church, the inner Spirit. She descends out of heaven and comes from God. This soul lost her self and is a new creature in Jesus Christ and is fit for this spiritual marriage. This Spouse is the soul made one in unity.

This is also spoken of the Church, filled with life, revived in its members. She is the Lamb's wife.

Rev. 21:11: ... having the glory of God. Her brilliance was like a very costly stone, as a stone of crystal-clear jasper.

This light and brilliance is a renewal of the Spirit, light and purity. Up till now she did not show her light. But now they appear with such a brightness that no one will ignore her light. The new Jerusalem, the Spouse, descends from heaven. All clouds have vanished. Truth was hidden under shadows but it is going to rise like a beautiful dawn, scattering all darkness and showing all the objects which could not be distinguished in the night.

Rev. 21:12-14: It had a great and high wall, with twelve gates, and at the gates twelve angels; and names were written on them, which are those of the twelve tribes of the sons of Israel. There were three gates on the east and three gates on the north and three gates on the south and three gates on the west. And the wall of the city had twelve foundation stones, and on them were the twelve names of the twelve apostles of the Lamb.

The Jewish people, so loved and cherished by God, whom God very greatly favored with so many miracles, from whom came so many patriarchs, holy prophets and martyrs, and from whom Jesus Christ even wished to be born, where the Church was born, the twelve apostles even being Jews—this people must not be regarded as being rejected forever. But the time for His mercy is very near and the Jews will again become the Saints of God.

He exercises a similar righteousness on souls who seem to have been chosen from the cradle, like the Jews were, to whom He seems to have given the grace of the old patriarchs in visions, revelations, and prophecy. However, afterward, these souls who seemed prodigies are rejected. Why? Because they became proud of themselves, attributing to themselves what was God's. And God rejects them in His righteousness while He takes other sinful souls who like the

Gentiles seem to be born in corruption and sin. These wandering ones He chooses to become thrones of mercy. However, God's mercy is so great that, though He permits these falls, He does not forsake them completely and brings them back in the latter part of their lives.

This wonderful city is the Church. After her renewal, it will have gates to receive the twelve tribes of Israel; and not them only but all the nations of the earth.

The wall is Jesus Christ Himself, keeping her and surrounding her everywhere. Its twelve gates show that there will be entrances on every side for the world; from everywhere children will come to her. None will be shut, signifying that there is no country, no nation that is not received in her bosom, especially the Jews who, scattered everywhere in the world, will be recalled in a marvelous way. The wall is simply Jesus Christ Himself. It is one wall and this shows the perfect oneness of the Church which being composed of so many stones is one single wall. The stones are living stones, according to the Scriptures, showing that the union is not outward but that of the hearts and minds, and that is what God wants. The true spirit is one of worship and sacrifice – an inner spirit.

The spirit of the apostles was an inner spirit of peace, union and unity, imparted by Jesus Christ. That Spirit, Jesus Christ wants to impart anew to His Church.

The Church's twelve gates indicate that she has freedom, breadth, and space. She was narrow and hindered formerly. The foundations of this wall are the twelve fruits of the Spirit, because she is full of them. The only stay is perfect love, the cornerstone – Jesus Christ.

> Rev. 21:15,16: And the one who spoke with me had a gold measuring rod to measure the city, and its gates and its wall. And the city is laid out as a square, and its length is as great as the width; and he measured the city with the rod, fifteen hundred miles; its length and width and height are equal.

The foursquare denotes the perfect equality there must be in everything. The whole soul, the whole Church, is one, so that what is done outside comes from within. The measure of each side is "twelve thousand furlongs," which shows a great extension, since the soul – and true Church – is in the immensity of God. My God, how great are these mysteries and how unexplainable!

This square indicates the equality and uniformity of the Church, enclosing everybody and being only enclosed in the immensity of God Himself. Oh, temple! Oh, Church, wonderful in yourself but too greatly humiliated by the unruliness of your children and because the shepherds and those leading you are fallen (not from their faith, but from the purity and holiness that such a holy ministry requires of them). A time will come when your shepherds are holy! But now, oh God, how corrupt are the priests and the shepherds! But the Lamb will make priests for Himself; He will make His saints!

Rev. 21:17: And he measured its wall, seventy-two years, according to human measurements, which are also angelic measurements.

The wall measured shows that the church will communicate its yieldedness to the movings of the Holy Spirit, to all nations.

Rev. 21:18: And the material of the wall was jasper; and the city was pure gold, like clear glass.

This shows the inner and outward likenesses of both the Church and the individual soul. For the Church, her ways are beautiful, firm, strong and pure, like the "jasper wall." The Spirit of the Church is so pure and clear that the Holy Spirit sees Himself portrayed there! She receives His rays so that the Spirit of the Church is the Holy Spirit filling, moving and leading her. As for her, she is led, ruled and enlightened without showing any resistance. The spirit of the Church will be outpoured on all her children. This city is pure gold; this denotes her sublime love. This gold is clear and transparent to receive the brilliance of the light of the Holy Spirit which is simplicity and spotlessness.

But what of the soul in this picture? She appears beautiful and strong, for God establishes her at last in a perfect inner and outward rest, with all the virtues and strength He seemed to have stripped her of, to perfect her in Him. After so many states of nothingness the soul has gone through, He gives the soul a wonderful consistency. Within the soul

155

is unmixed gold because of a pure love, unmixed by self-interest. It is a very pure glass because of her simplicity and candor that hides nothing.

> **Rev. 21:19-21: The foundation stones of the city wall were adorned with every kind of precious stone. The first foundation stone was jasper; the second, sapphire; the third, chalcedony; the fourth, emerald; the fifth, sardonyx; the sixth, sardius; the seventh, chrysolite; the eighth, beryl; the ninth, topaz; the tenth, chrysoprase; the eleventh, jacinth; the twelfth, amethyst. And the twelve gates were twelve pearls; each one of the gates was a single pearl. And the street of the city was pure gold, like transparent glass.**

"The foundations of the wall" are the main essentials of the faith on which this soul bases its conduct, and it is so also for the Church. All is enriched with precious stones, the purest virtues.

The pearls which are the twelve gates show the purity of the inner life, the uniformity in all souls, the uniformity of faith and feelings, always the same, changing only to become purer. The walls in which are the twelve gates speak also of uniformity in their shape and
component and although all kinds of people are received through these gates such as the Jews, the bad Christians, they will enter the city, share its spirit, will become inwardly led, and be placed in the truth.

> **Rev. 21:22: And I saw no temple in it, for the Lord God, the Almighty, and the Lamb, are its temple.**

This cannot be applied to the Church; however we can say that He Himself is "the temple," the sacrifice and the victim.

Formerly the soul had a temple within itself where it withdrew, prayed and worshipped. This temple was a place of refuge where the soul was in safety, protected from the oppression of its enemies. Now, there is no more temple in the soul, for her temple is God Himself, in a manner that can be better experienced than described.

Rev. 21:23: And the city has no need of the sun or of the moon to shine upon it, for the glory of God has illumined it, and its lamp is the Lamb.

The Church has no need of any created light; God alone is her light and so is the Lamb.

As for the soul, it has no more need of illustrations.

In this case, there are no more distinct lights, God being the general light. By the favor of this general light the soul sees all things in God in a wonderful way. This is the way the blessed ones see.

Rev. 21:24-27: And the nations shall walk by its light, and the kings of the earth shall bring their glory into it. And in the daytime (for there shall be no night there) its gates shall never be closed; and they shall bring the glory and the honor of the nations into it; and nothing unclean and no one who practices abomination and lying, shall ever come into it, but only those whose names are written in the Lamb's book of life.

The nations shall walk in the light of the truth and the Church, and they will come to join them. Then the mind and will of man being entirely united to God's, there will be no more false light causing them to go astray; but divine light will enlighten them all.

All the kings of the earth and sovereigns will place their honor in the service of God's interest alone, for His glory only. The gates of the Church shall not be shut at all to anybody because there will be no darkness, no night. This is why God will have such an onslaught to destroy all enemies, so that nothing impure will be received in this pure and clean Church.

Likewise the soul in God is so completely spoiled that any impurity will be taken from her, for in God, nothing impure enters.

22

Rev. 22:1: And he showed me a river of the water of life, clear as crystal, coming from the throne of God and of the Lamb ...

This river is the grace of God that continuously flows from out of Him into souls. This river is the abyss where all souls are lost and sunk in His unity. It proceeds out of the throne of God and of the Lamb, because it is given by God Himself and by Jesus Christ.

Rev. 22:2: ... in the middle of its street. And on either side of the river was the tree of life, bearing twelve kinds of fruit, yielding its fruit every month; and the leaves of the tree were for the healing of the nations.

The tree of life is perfect love in the Church and in the soul. This love is burning, pure and always dwells in the soul. This tree has twelve fruits which are fruits of the Holy Spirit appearing in their season and according to the soul's need. The leaves represent the most common graces distributed to men to heal them from their ailments. Oh Church, this tree is given you. Nevertheless the nations do not eat of it and this is why they are not healed. But as soon as the people come to you, they will be nourished, refreshed and healed. These fruits and this tree are ever in the Church.

Rev. 22:3,4: And there shall no longer be any curse; and the throne of God and of the Lamb shall be in

it, and His bond-servants shall serve Him; and they shall see His face, and His name shall be on their foreheads.

This sight of God's face may be taken for a close union. When the soul has reached this intimate fellowship, it sees the face of the Lamb because of the deep knowledge of Jesus Christ given her.

The name of the Lamb is written on their foreheads, means that their outward appearance is a proof of what they feel within. Their exterior even preaches and announces God.

Rev. 22:5: And there shall no longer be any night; and they shall not have need of the light of a lamp nor the light of the sun, because the Lord God shall illumine them; and they shall reign forever and ever.

In this place, there can be no night because the light of the truth makes room for no darkness.

This will happen for the Church of God. In proportion as the darkness of error and of falsehood passes away, truth will appear as it is and the light will scatter darkness.

Rev. 22:6,7: And he said to me, "These words are faithful and true"; and the Lord, the God of the spirits of the prophets, sent His angel to show to His bond-servants the things which must shortly take place. And behold, I am coming quickly. Blessed is he who heeds the words of the prophecy of this book."

Oh God, this is the joy of the hearts that are wholly, unreservedly yours. Your inner and outward reign will come and these sayings are faithful and true. Oh God, You are going to reign in every heart and You already do in thousands of them. This is ignored by those who do not feel this way, but it is known to God and to the soul to whom He manifests Himself. Oh God of spirits, You gave Your inner Spirit to John so that he could clearly speak of inner things, Your general work in the souls You want to unite to Yourself forever.

But oh, holy prophet, you say that these things must shortly be done. Alas! Seventeen centuries have passed since then!* The reign of Jesus has not yet come throughout the earth. There are more inner persons in this century than there ever were.† You say, Lord, that You are coming. Alas, oh Lord, how long this waiting time seems! But for You centuries are a moment. Oh, desired of nations, You made Yourself to be longed for, for four thousand years. As the prophets spoke, Your day seemed near. However, how delayed it was! You make Yourself to be desired of so many souls who sigh after Your reign and You do not come! Pardon me, oh King, You are coming. You came to reign in thousands of hearts in an unknown way, and in eternity we will see how this inner spirit spread in every century and increased each day. But You have not come, oh Jesus, in all the extent of Your reign, to make Yourself known in this manner to all the earth. Oh God, this is Your way of doing, to intensify our desire and try Your servants' patience.

As soon as God begins to come into a soul, He promises that one will be His Spouse. He has her desire this eagerly, as we see in Solomon's Song. It seems the marriage is going to take place at the outset, but alas! the nearer it seems, the farther it is. The soul, seeing the favors and kindnesses of the Bridegroom, believes she has only one step to take and she will be in the Bride's company. She thinks she has reached the height of perfection, yet she has hardly started. She realizes after a long and terrible experience that such a great attainment is not so close at hand. Then she says to her God: You promised to come just now and as soon as You promised, You fled farther than ever! Oh, how the moments spent before God become long and laborious years! Oh Love, You do not deceive. The creature deceives and believes she can be admitted to the marriage, without leaving the robes of her captivity. Oh, what a mistake she makes! And how foolish she is when she finds it so hard to let herself be stripped! This lengthens her torment and the greater the resistance to the Spouse's will, the harder, too, her sorrow. However, oh sacred Spouse, "You come soon" if we consider what You are and the vileness of this creature

* Twenty centuries, now!
† And less, in our age!

160

to whom You desire to unite Yourself. You do not delay this fine gift.

"Blessed are those who keep the sayings of the prophecy of this book." How fortunate are those who fulfill these words though they are apparently met with many calamities.

> **Rev. 22:8,9: And I, John, am the one who heard and saw these things. And when I heard and saw, I fell down to worship at the feet of the angel who showed me these things. And he said to me, "Do not do that; I am a fellow servant of yours and of your brethren the prophets and of those who heed the words of this book; worship God."**

God took a delight in hiding His treasures in earthen vessels, so that the power may be regarded as of God and not of men. He knows the beauty and nobility of this soul covered with outward mud. God allows this to keep them in their purity and to prevent them from being overestimated if they were known. We should look to God alone.

> **Rev. 22:10,11: And he said to me, "Do not seal up the words of the prophecy of this book, for the time is near. Let the one who does wrong, still do wrong; and let the one who is filthy, still be filthy; and let the one who is righteous, still practice righteousness; and let the one who is holy, still keep himself holy."**

Here two kinds of people are spoken of, those who are unrighteous and those who feel their own wretchedness. In the first case, sin and the punishment by more sin is being referred to. For the second, a state of distress and weakness is shown, God hiding man through these both from Himself and from others. Oh God, this man mourns his misery; he knows he can't help himself by his efforts and that You alone can heal him. He grieves, not only on account of his humiliation but also for fear of displeasing You.

"He that is holy, let him be holy still": that is, let him be transformed into the holiness of God, losing completely his own.

Rev. 22:12,13: "Behold, I am coming quickly, and My reward is with Me, to render to every man according to what he has done. I am the Alpha and the Omega, the first and the last, the beginning and the end." Blessed are those who wash their robes, that they may have the right to the tree of life, and may enter by the gates into the city.

Oh God, You come quickly because You are righteous and also because You are merciful. The works which are accepted are done in Your will. The work of a plain man in his shop who is united in God's will shall appear exceedingly more precious than many works which appear great before men and that have for principle only the love of glory, self interest, and the will of man. You do not look at the greatness of the action but at the intention with which it is done, and at the purity of man's love. "The Alpha and Omega" means the principle of the inner way and the consummation, the perfection of this same inner life. You are the principle from which everything starts and You are the end where everything ends. We begin and end by You.

Some persons have thought that we must always meditate on Jesus Christ. They are mistaken. The point is not considering Jesus Christ, and discussing Jesus Christ, but being led by Him in every way, and being truly possessed by Him. Reasoning does not give these things. Abandonment does. A friend is not known by reasoning. You can never know someone as a friend and neglect associating with him!

Jesus Christ is the great book written within and without. What is within is exceedingly more than what appears. He alone can manifest what He is to the soul. He does this not by reasoning but by the impression He gives the soul about Himself and His states. Paul expresses this when he says he bears in his body the marks of Jesus Christ. Paul does not say he reasons about Jesus Christ. He says, "I bear His state." Then he admits he does not live his own life but Jesus Christ lives in him because he denied himself, became nothing in the hands of God. He allowed Him to destroy his own self life to make room for the life of Jesus Christ.

Rev. 22:14,15: Blessed are those who wash their robes, that they may have the right to the tree of

life, and may enter by the gates into the city. Outside are the dogs and the sorcerers and the immoral persons and the murderers and the idolaters, and everyone who loves and practices lying.

"Blessed are they that wash their robes," refers to the dear souls who, by a complete abandonment and trust, throw themselves in the arms of God, giving themselves to Him so as to be purified. These souls, who are persuaded of their extreme poverty and helplessness, throw themselves into this immense sea of the blood of Jesus Christ without any hesitation. Oh, how well purified are these!

Rev. 22:16: "I, Jesus, have sent My angel to testify to you these things for the churches. I am the root and the offspring of David, the bright morning star."

Oh Jesus, name that charms and stirs, name of joy and salvation, You always send Your angel before You "to testify" of You. This angel appeared, but it is not enough; Jesus Christ must appear.

The Church saw this angel, and soon she will see her Spouse. As the morning star precedes the daylight and sunrise, so Jesus comes first to the soul as the bright and morning star before she is placed in the full daylight of Glory.

When the soul seems to have lost sight of Him, being sunk in the immensity of God, then Jesus Christ springs forth and communicates Himself to the soul in such a wonderful way that she grows and is surprisingly fruitful.

Rev. 22:17: And the Spirit and the bride say, "Come." And let the one who hears say, "Come." And let the one who is thirsty come; let the one who wishes take the water of life without cost.

"The Spirit and the Bride say: Come," to Jesus. This Spirit and this Bride are the Holy Spirit and the Church. The Church united to the Holy Spirit and animated by this Spirit asks Jesus Christ to come and reign quickly.

The truth which is with the Spirit invites the Bridegroom to come; she cannot do anything after appearing on earth and wants to see the second advent that has been described.

"The Spirit and the Bride say: Come." We must know that the soul in God has no prayer of her own any longer, but the Holy Spirit prays in her with inexpressible groanings. The Spirit and Bride, of one accord, with one voice and one prayer, invite Him to come.

They invite Him much more to come to His Church and make Himself known in all the earth, possessing His reign, manifesting His truth. The Spirit and Church say: Come, oh the desired of nations, come, joy and satisfaction of people, come to put an end to their misfortune and to start their happiness. Come to reign as a Sovereign. Come to consummate Your marriage. Come, oh Jesus, come to be King!

After the desire of the Spirit and the Bride has been expressed, Jesus, this Bridegroom of the souls, invites all thirsty souls to come and quench their thirst at these calm and quiet waters, to this water that nourishes and refreshes him who drinks. Oh Christians, my brothers, it is easier to have life than you realize. You only have to "come" to Jesus simply and trustfully, and He will give you the fullness of life. He says: Let him that is athirst come and rivers of living water will flow to everlasting life. The believer who gives himself to Jesus Christ, goes to Him, feels (after his thirst is quenched at this divine source) that he is made also a spring where others come to quench their thirst.

Rev. 22:18,19: I testify to everyone who hears the words of the prophecy of this book: if anyone adds to them, God shall add to him the plagues which are written in this book; and if anyone takes away from the words of the book of this prophecy, God shall take away his part from the tree of life and from the holy city, which are written in this book.

John describes in this book all the states through which God brings the souls. He omits nothing. Anyone who would produce other states different from these would go astray. He who would certify that these states are not real would be presumptuous and not fit to feel such divine and real things. Some people condemn all they don't understand; but they do not judge God right by measuring His goodness by their reasonings! Let all who doubt put Him to the test and they will see that the goodness of God for souls goes beyond all that can be said.

Rev. 22:20,21: He who testifies to these things says, "Yes, I am coming quickly." Amen. Come, Lord Jesus. The grace of the Lord Jesus be with all. Amen.

Oh Jesus, You promise it, You assure it is so. Yet though Your word is true, You delay Your coming so! Oh, how this delay is long for a heart who loves You, who only wants Your glory and who only wishes to see You reign in every heart and everywhere! Come, then, oh my King, come and begin Your reign. Do not delay any more! Come then, Lord Jesus! May the grace of our Lord prepare us all for this second advent. Amen!

THE
BOOK
OF
JAMES
EXCERPTS

JAMES

Excerpts from Mme Guyon's commentary on the book of James

> **James 1:1–4:** James, a bond-servant of God and of the Lord Jesus Christ, to the twelve tribes who are dispersed abroad, greetings. Consider it all joy, my brethren, when you encounter various trials, knowing that the testing of your faith produces endurance. And let endurance have its perfect result, that you may be perfect and complete, lacking in nothing.

If you see suffering from God's point of view – which is the proper view – you will appreciate having these afflictions, and will consider it your greatest joy to have many of them. James says that the test of your faith produces endurance, or patience. Affliction is your real test of faith. Faith is gold, purified by the fire of love. Faith is made pure by love, but is tested by affliction.

What advantage is there in the testing of your faith? James tells us. A work is perfect when it is so in its beginning, its development, and its ending. It must be perfect inwardly and outwardly. No exceptions. Inward patience watches all God's work as it proceeds within, bearing with the sweet, and the bitter. Inward patience is the most difficult of all. It is easier to bear, with a constant perseverance, all outward torments, than to bear with an equal patience all inward workings. So even though this patience does not extend to all the transforming work of God, it is good — because whatever we suffer inwardly from God is a good thing, whether painful or sweet.

This patience can only be considered perfect when it will bear with all the ways of God continuously. He who is agreeing with the dealings of God is praying passively, whether for a few moments or longer. But he is only perfectly passive when he is without resistance, even without aversion; for when resistance begins, aversion follows. Only this kind of patience, when joined to outward patience, makes the work perfect.

Some view this state of inner patience as a frightful monster. Those without understanding rise against those who choose to bear the divine ways, considering them to be deceived. However, self-deception will not come to a person who bears things which are heavenly, with a perfect and constant attitude, but rather to one who wants to oversee his own transformation, or to suffer only some of what God has for him. Those who want to be in control of divine things, giving them a pleasing form, are likely to be deceived, because the devil and self are able to imitate these divine things. Instead of suffering divine things, we seek them out of curiosity, or even worse, out of pride and self-love.

Those who desire only pleasing things and not the crucifying ways are also in danger of being deceived because through this preference, they refuse that which will cause them to bear the image of the Son of God. Satan transforms himself into an angel of light, so as to print in them his own image, deceiving them with what is satisfying and excellent in appearance only. But the one who inwardly suffers divine things cannot be deceived when he suffers them all, without any preference.

We said that a work is perfect when it is so in its beginning, and all the way through. A work is perfect in its start when the soul is bearing the dealings of God Who is the author of every perfection, and the principle of it. It is perfect in its operation, since God is the one in control. It is perfect in its end, since this is the end a perfect God has chosen. It is the man's interference that causes imperfection in a work. The patient man chooses not to interfere in what God does in his life, not even to the extent of seeing it, feeling it, or knowing it; he remains prostrated, resigned, abandoned to all His will, so that God can do with His creature whatever He wills. The demon can enter only through the senses, which do not interfere when the soul remains utterly resigned; he must not be afraid of being deceived, because his patience knows no bounds.

As the operations coming from God aim only at the destruction of self and all that pertains to it, surrendering all to God, the soul that bears these destructive operations cannot be deceived. That soul does not aim at being taken up by anything, such as graces, gifts, or favors, having gradually died to these things, and then remaining dead. Then God alone is this soul's principle and perfection; His operation is perfect in this person's submission and dependency on God, and God's will. Having no other end than God, His will and His glory, he will be perfect when God has finished His work.

True passivity, when perfect, does not consist in doing nothing, as some have mistakenly imagined; it consists in allowing Him who leads and governs us, to do in us and with us what He pleases. Is this being passive and suffering His working, if we do not let Him move us in order to participate in His work? Suffering what is being done to us is a type of patience. A more perfect, nobler patience is allowing Him to do with us what He wants, and in the way He wants, and working according to the moving of Him who moves us. Some, under the pretext of being passive, do not wish to move. This must not be our way. God must be allowed to do His work. To resist God in a thing He wants to do by us is as great an evil as resisting Him in what He wants to do in us, isn't it?

At first God's dealings aim only at defeating the ways of man, so that He may become the principle of our actions, and allow patience to have a perfect work, as James says. Patience and passivity do not come naturally to us at first; we want to be doing something. We have misunderstood the words, "Faith without works is dead." Far from being patient, we resist and reject patience, because of a strong self-love, and a hidden confidence in ourselves and our own work. We resist God, not submitting to His working; we become the guiding force of our own works. Although the grace of God is empowering the little good we do, self interferes powerfully. Grace seems to enter into action like the school teacher, who is forced, by the hand of the child he wanted to help, to form a very imperfect handwriting. If the child had allowed the teacher to direct his hand, every letter would have been perfect. When we do not yield to God's hand, we try to succeed by our own efforts. We think we have won a victory when we have done much; it seems to us that God, who usually does not go against our freedom, has surrendered to us!

It is easy to see that we must go contrary to our natural ways and yield to God, so that our works will be perfect. This is the kingdom of Jesus Christ, without which we cannot do the will of God. The reign of God must come in us; this means He must lead and govern us as He pleases, so that His will may be done. If not, His will shall never be done; it will really be our own will. Then the first passivity on our part, although imperfect in the beginning, must be to yield our ways to God, little by little, and to allow Him to take over. For a long time, the soul possesses only a shadow of passivity, often acting more than God, then as much as God, and only gradually allowing God a wider scope to work as our patience becomes stronger – till finally He takes over.

The first dealings of God, then, serve only to break down our strong natural inclinations. And the first patience required of us is to allow God to do this. Jesus Christ calls this "denying one's self." Paul refers to it as "being led by the Spirit"; and David speaks of hearing what the Lord will speak (Psalms 85:8).

The second degree of passivity shows that the soul, through patience, has renounced its ways, and remains dead, without action. It bears God's dealings with a free and willing submission. Its perfect resignation consists in allowing God to do what He wills in a dead and renounced soul. But before this takes place, that soul remains in this dying state a long time; it takes over and then lets go, till that person does not feel or taste or distinguish his own submission and resignation, nor the advancement of the kingdom of Jesus Christ. He does all that is wanted without thinking that he is yielding to the will of God, with complete oblivion of self. God raises him or puts him down, and his patience remains the same. His own life, through death, has taken up and absorbed life. And this ends the third degree of God's dealings.

This believer not only resigns himself to God, letting God do with him and in him all He wants without resistance; he is now also becoming alive again with the life that God has given him; he undertakes actions which appear entirely divine, of which God alone is the author. He does the will of God constantly, unerringly, and at the same time so freely and easily that these actions seem entirely genuine.

As a living man lives without thinking of his life, so does such a one, allowing God to move within, live God's life. Divine life is more natural to him than his own life was, and he is passive, letting God work, remaining dead to any act except that of God, allowing Him to do with him and in him what pleases God. Moreover, he is alive with God's life; he acts and works in God. This is no longer a dying state, or a dead one, but a living condition, full of infinite freedom. Nothing limits this soul; he never wonders how he will do God's will, yet that will is always done; he does it without ceasing since he has surrendered his own will for God's. All he wants is God's will; all he does, God does it.

There we see perfection, and the accomplishment of all passivity. Jesus Christ works, not through a body which He would change and beautify, but through a body which He owns. In such a state we are really His members, His children. He is our God. We are His images, with more advantages than when God first created man in His own image. In this soul, at last, He takes delight.

But what life does this person live? Isn't it extraordinary? No. A life which appears to be extraordinary is not desired. A life filled with love, genuine, artless, harmless; a life that is real and true, not having to die any longer: such a life will be broad, free, and entirely godly. But some will say, "That soul is sinless." True, he sins with great difficulty, and few have reached that place. Usually small faults occur unwillingly, and do not wound the heart of the Bridegroom.

These are the degrees of passivity which make us perfect in every work, as far as inner life is concerned. As for the outward life, which draws its perfection from the interior life: When the inner patience is perfect, the outer patience will also be perfect.

There are three kinds of inward sufferings. The first are those caused by resisting, and through greed. These will cease as soon as we yield to God and do what He wants us to. We then see that these trials came because of our resistance. The second sufferings are purifying; by them God purifies the soul of blemishes. They end when what God wanted to purify is done. The third kind of suffering is sent by God so that we will be conformed to the image of His Son. This is the portion only of those who have denied themselves, and resist no longer.

Outward patience allows us to bear all that happens to us from God through His providence, from people through their mistakes and meanness, and from ourselves through our weaknesses, follies, defects and distresses. The first, those coming from God, include poverty, hunger, cold, sicknesses, accidents, and misfortunes of any kind. The sufferings coming through other people are such as slander, persecutions, vexations, wrong dealings, and losses of property and reputation. Finally sufferings come to us through our defects and imperfections. This kind of suffering extends everywhere and requires a general patience which will show, more than anything else, the holiness of the soul. Therefore the Lord said, "In your patience possess ye your souls." How is this done? He Himself explains it when He says, "Whosoever will save his life shall lose it." Possessing one's soul means to be master of one's soul; only in God do we truly possess our souls, and only there do we find total loss which can give us a perfect patience.

The patient soul, possessing such complete patience, has reached all the perfection that can be had in this life, and is lacking nothing. If something is lacking, he has not reached the full development of the patience he needs.

James 3:1,2: Let not many of you become teachers, my brethren, knowing that as such we shall incur a stricter judgment. For we all stumble in many ways. If anyone does not stumble in what he says, he is a perfect man, able to bridle the whole body as well.

When the heart is pure, plain, simple, so are the words. To be pure with the tongue, we must be pure in heart. Such purity of heart can only come from within. A person who is only occupied with his God within, in the center of his soul, and who is not thinking of holding his tongue, realizes that his tongue is kept and directed by the One Who directs his heart. His solitude inwardly makes him keep a silence, outwardly, which is full of cheerfulness without pretence.

Others trouble everybody with their outward and affected moderation. But those directed by God are courteous and easily pleased. Without displeasing God, they know how to be without offense toward anyone, which is a grace for mature Christians. But those who have not come into the liberty of the children of God, are in bondage. They bring those around them into bondage as well, by making godliness seem unpleasant. Jesus Christ was kind to all. The austere and troublesome Pharisees were offended. A believer in whom Jesus Christ lives and reigns is conciliating, and though he may not please all, he is not burdensome.

Then God should keep the tongue, and in order to do so, He must govern our heart. David does not say, "I will keep my tongue;" instead he says, "Set a watch before my mouth."

> James 3:3-8: Now if we put the bits into the horses' mouths so that they may obey us, we direct their entire body as well. Behold, the ships also, though they are so great and are driven by strong winds, are still directed by a very small rudder, wherever the inclination of the pilot desires. So also the tongue is a small part of the body, and yet it boasts of great things. Behold, how great a forest is set aflame by such a small fire! And the tongue is a fire, the very world of iniquity; the tongue is set among our members as that which defiles the entire body, and sets on fire the course of our life, and is set on fire by hell. For every species of beasts and birds, of reptiles and creatures of the sea, is tamed, and has been tamed by the human race. But no one can tame the tongue; it is a restless evil and full of deadly poison.

If governing the tongue is so crucial, yet so difficult to accomplish, and if this small monster is so fierce and unmanageable, it is obvious that some mightier force must direct it, and prevent it from doing damage. A ship is being led and governed, though it is pushed by violent winds. In the same manner, the tongue must be led in spite of its boisterousness. But who must govern it? Isn't it man who, you say, tamed the wildest animals? He will very easily direct such a small thing, won't he? Yet James assures us that this tongue, being more unmanageable than the most fierce and powerful animals, cannot be tamed by man. Another must do so, or the poor tongue will remain uncontrollable. It must be tamed, otherwise it will direct everything and be led by no one. Yet its owner is more criminal by it than by anything else.

Oh, what a strong argument in favor of the inward life! You have in you, my brothers, an excellent Pilot who knows how to handle and lead your tongue which is unmanageable to anyone else. Make Him the owner of it, and in a moment He will make it powerless and use it as He pleases. It will be made a tool, not for evil, but for His glory and praise. And how will you place it in His hands? By making Him the master of your heart and of your whole being, abandoning yourself to Him unreservedly.

When God is absolute master of the heart, the tongue only says what God makes it say. When God rules over our heart, only good things come out of this heart. But when Satan is in our heart, he leads our tongue as he pleases; he sets it all on fire; he pours everywhere the poison of hell: quarrels, lies, backbitings, and blasphemies. It is easy to judge that the devil governs the tongue which says such things. It is also easy to understand that when the tongue speaks only for God, and for the neighbor's good, God governs it. The tongue is a very small helm. It is easy to notice, seeing the way it goes, who is the owner of the ship, Jesus Christ or the devil.

> **James 3:9–12: With it we bless our Lord and Father; and with it we curse men, who have been made in the likeness of God; from the same mouth come both blessing and cursing. My brethren, these things ought not to be this way. Does a fountain send out from the same opening both fresh and bitter water? Can a fig tree, my brethren, produce olives, or a vine produce figs? Neither can salt water produce fresh.**

These words show us the importance of the heart. When the heart is well governed, so is the tongue; and when the heart is badly governed, the tongue is depraved. When the heart is full of God, only excellent waters can flow from such a good spring; when it is filled with the devil, only bitter and poisoned waters will come forth. How can this mouth say anything good? Usually it does not. Sometimes the sinner stops being a sinner, briefly turning to God, then returning to the devil. Such a condition comes also from the habit of praying without fervor or thoughtlessly. God is not in such hearts. Such people mumble and do not pray.

> **James 3:13–15: Who among you is wise and understanding? Let him show by his good behavior his deeds in the gentleness of wisdom. But if you have bitter jealousy and selfish ambition in your heart, do not be arrogant and so lie against the truth. This wisdom is not that which comes down from above, but is earthly, natural, demonic.**

Those who aim at being perfect must be kind, easily entreated, and yielding, keeping still rather than quarreling. It is hard to believe how much these strong quarrels impair the spirit of love, soil the soul, and strengthen stubbornness and self-sufficiency. Though the one we quarrel with may have a wrong opinion, he will never be won through contending. On the contrary, he becomes bitter and hardened, whereas by kindness, without controversy, he may be won. As soon as agitation appears, it is better to stop the debate; death to ourselves is more useful than all we could do through this life of self, which truly shows itself in such arguments; for as zeal comes, bitterness also enters into both parties, and instead of being united in feelings, we are separated at heart. Yielding to others, submitting in everything except our faith, is a necessary virtue. Losing is gain, and he who yields is the most enlightened, because he knows how to master self.

> **James 3:16: For where jealousy and selfish ambition exist, there is disorder and every evil thing.**

Let us keep our feelings to ourselves unless they may be useful and shared with meekness. If there is any resistance, let us wait for a more favorable time. Showing patience and humbleness of heart will convince others more about the truth we tell them, than any controversy would.

> **James 3:17,18: But the wisdom from above is first pure, then peaceable, gentle, reasonable, full of mercy and good fruits, unwavering, without hypocrisy. And the seed whose fruit is righteousness is sown in peace by those who make peace.**

The truly wise ones, endowed with the wisdom of Jesus Christ, speak with peace, meekness, and gentleness; the fire of sacred love merely adds a certain liveliness to their speech which comes from a full heart, and gives more grace to their words, showing the abundance of the speaker. This fire comes from heaven and imparts sweetness, unlike the fire of quarreling, coming from hell, which is full of bitterness. The one who is possessed of the wisdom that gives peace is always ready to yield to all (except in that which is not faith), believing that others know more, and have more experience. Even when he knows perfectly the matters that are discussed, he is pleased to share his thoughts peacefully. If what he says is contended, he remains quiet, leaving it to God to enlighten and make the truth known.

This wisdom teaches more by example than by words, because it is simple. He who is simple, not complicated, thinks evil of no one. He sees everything right; and when actions are questioned, he lets God be the judge. Nothing displeases God as much as rash judgments. The one who judges his brother steps on God's rights; usually he makes a mistake, and thinks that good is evil. Some people, on a mere suspicion, are quick to accuse their brother. We cannot stress too much the greatness of this evil, coming usually from a conscience that is not straight. Those who do not walk straight believe that everybody is like them. This does not refer to the knowledge God gives on the condition of souls that have to be corrected. This refers to judgments and evil suspicions on the simplest and clearest actions. Finally James adds that those who love peace with their brothers and God, sow fruits of righteousness in this peace.

CONCLUSION

CONCLUSION

(This is a conclusion to all her commentary on the Bible)

I beg those who will read this and do not have experience of the inner ways, not to condemn but to refer to persons who have the experience, and try to have this experience themselves. Let us not find such sublime states so strange. God wanted it this way and it is all enclosed in the Holy Scriptures. I affirm not to have used any book besides the Bible alone, not having read any Father of the Church. I only used the Scriptures, with faith, as I wrote all that came to my mind promptly, without thinking of it or meditating to see if what I was writing was good. I never re-read it in order to make corrections. I leave this work as it is in the hands of my Director to do with it as he pleases and as God will inspire him.

The grace I am asking You, oh loving God, is to make Yourself known, enjoyed, loved by all who will read this. If through my own weakness I inserted terms that are not suitable, this does not prevent the truth of the foundation. Make Yourself known, oh God; make Yourself to be loved. No one will ever love You as You ought unless he abandons himself to You and You give him Your love.

It is surprising that everybody who reads the Scriptures will not discover the delightful and wonderful beauty of the interior life which is sown there in such a clear way. There is no place where it is not described. All kinds of people will find in these explanations, here or there, what they need. The Proverbs have what is necessary for a beginner and "Ecclesiastes" still more. In all kinds of places, the leadings of God for the soul will be seen, and His intricate ways for anyone.

You, oh God, are the author of the good in this work. It seems I only lent my hand, but it may have been, at times, unfaithful, and so it will be easy to notice that the evil comes from my weakness. The rest is Yours, oh God. It comes from You. I return it and have no part in it. Oh God, use it as You wish. If You want it for the good of Your Church, manifest it.

September 23, 1683

CHRISTIAN BOOKS PUBLISHING HOUSE

BOOKS BY GENE EDWARDS

THE DIVINE ROMANCE

The most powerful, arresting book we have ever published. With a might and beauty that sweeps from eternity to eternity, here is, truly, the greatest love story ever told. If you have any interest at all in the deeper Christian life, then, by all means, read this book. Rarely, if ever, has the depth and mystery of Christ been put so simply, yet so profoundly and so breathtakingly beautiful.

A TALE OF THREE KINGS

A book beloved around the world. A dramatically told tale of Saul, David and Absalom, on the subject of brokenness. A book used in the healing of the lives of many Christians who have been devastated by church splits and by injuries suffered at the hands of other Christians.

OUR MISSION

A group of Christian young men in their early twenties met together for a weekend retreat to hear Gene Edwards speak. Unknown to them, they were about to pass through a catastrophic split. These messages were delivered to prepare those young men spiritually for the inevitable disaster facing them. Edwards presents the standard of the first century believers and how those believers walked when passing through similar crises. A remarkable statement on how a Christian is to conduct himself in times of strife, division and crisis. A book every Christian, every minister, every worker will need at one time or another in his life.

INWARD JOURNEY

Crossing time and space, a young man named Chris Young learns the Christian meaning of transformation. A study in suffering, pain and the ways of God in our lives.

LETTERS TO A DEVASTATED CHRISTIAN

Gene Edwards writes a series of letters to a Christian who has been deeply damaged by a crisis in the group he has been part of. A book that has brought help, counsel and healing to many hurt Christians.

BOOKS BY MADAM GUYON

EXPERIENCING THE DEPTHS OF JESUS CHRIST

Guyon's first and best known book. One of the most influential pieces of Christian literature ever penned on the deeper Christian life. Among the multitudes of people who have read this book and urged others to read it are: John Wesley, Adoniram Judson, Watchman Nee, Jesse Penn-Lewis, Zinzendorf, and the Quakers. A timeless piece of literature that has been on the "must read" list of Christians for 300 years.

THE STORY OF MADAME GUYON'S LIFE, by T.C. Upham

If you enjoy reading Jeanne Guyon's writings, you will wish to read the story of her life. Through the centuries a multitude of Christians have held it to be the most outstanding life story of any Christian woman in church history. Truly one of Christendom's best known and most frequently read biographies.

Her well-known autobiography details her life only to about 40, whereas she became an internationally known figure and spiritual influence in Europe after that time. Some of the most significant aspects of her life story are not included in her remarkable autobiography. T.C. Upham's history of her life, on the other hand, recounts her fame in the Court of Louis XIV, her clash with Bossuet, her trial, the international storm created by Fenelon's clash with Bossuet over her teachings, her imprisonment in the dungeon of Vincennes, her four years as a prisoner in the infamous Bastille.

One of the half dozen truly great Christian biographies.

THE SPIRITUAL ADVENTURE

This book could well be called volume two of EXPERIENCING THE DEPTHS OF JESUS CHRIST. Here is a look at the experiences a more advanced and faithful Christian might encounter in his/her walk with the Lord. Without question, next to EXPERIENCING THE DEPTHS, here is Mme. Jeanne Guyon's best book.

UNION WITH GOD

Written as a companion book to EXPERIENCING THE DEPTHS OF JESUS CHRIST, and includes 22 of her poems.

SONG OF SONGS
GENESIS

Jeanne Guyon wrote a commentary on the Bible; here are two of those books. SONG OF SONGS has been popular through the centuries and has greatly influenced several other well-known commentaries on the Song of Songs.

THE SPIRITUAL LETTERS OF MADAME GUYON

Here is spiritual counseling at its very best. There is a Christ-centeredness to Jeanne Guyon's counsel that is rarely, if ever, seen in Christian literature.

THE WAY OUT

A spiritual study of Exodus as seen from "the interior way."

THE BOOK OF JOB

Guyon looks at the life of Job from the view of the deeper Christian life.

CHRIST OUR REVELATION

A profound and spiritual look at the book of Revelation.

CLASSICS ON THE DEEPER CHRISTIAN LIFE

PRACTICING HIS PRESENCE

The monumental seventeenth century classic by Brother Lawrence, now in modern English. One of the most read and recommended Christian books of the last 300 years.

The twentieth century missionary, Frank Laubach, while living in the

Philippines, sought to put into practice Brother Lawrence's words. Included in this edition are excerpts from Frank Laubach's diary. This book is a Christian classic by *any* standard; this book consistently shows up on more "top-ten must-read" book recommendations list than any other piece of Christian literature in print.

THE SPIRITUAL GUIDE

At the time Jeanne Guyon was teaching in the royal court of Louis XIV (in France), a man named Michael Molinos was leading a spiritual revival among the clergy and laymen of Rome! He actually lived in the Vatican, his influence reaching to all Italy and beyond. The great, the near great, the unknown sought him out for spiritual counsel. He was the spiritual director of many of the illuminaries of the seventeenth century. He wrote THE SPIRITUAL GUIDE to meet the need of a growing hunger for spiritual direction. The book was, for a time, probably the most popular book in Europe, but was later banned and condemned to be burned. The author was convicted and sentenced to a dungeon after one of the most sensational trials in European history.

Here, in modern English, is that remarkable book.

CHURCH HISTORY

These two books bring to bear a whole new perspective on church life.

THE EARLY CHURCH

This book tells, in a "you are there" approach, what it was like to be a Christian in the first century church, recounting the events from Pentecost to Antioch. By Gene Edwards.

THE TORCH OF THE TESTIMONY

John W. Kennedy tells the little known, almost forgotten, story of evangelical Christians during the dark ages.

If you are just getting acquainted with books on the deeper Christian life, we would like to suggest what may be the best approach to reading books on this subject. There is not a great deal of literature available in this area of the Christian walk, so you will wish to make the most of what is available.

We recommend that you begin your reading with THE DIVINE ROMANCE. Follow with EXPERIENCING THE DEPTHS OF JESUS CHRIST and PRACTICING HIS PRESENCE. THE DIVINE ROMANCE will stir and give insight and prepare you for the practical and spiritual help found in the other two books.

Two other books which complement EXPERIENCING THE DEPTHS OF JESUS CHRIST are UNION WITH GOD and THE SPIRITUAL GUIDE.

You will also find real profit in reading THE SPIRITUAL LETTERS of Jeanne Guyon and THE SPIRITUAL LETTERS of Fenelon. Many of the questions and problems of your daily walk with Christ and your relationship with others are dealt with in these two books.

For insight into brokenness and to see just what the heart of a man of God should be, the beautiful A TALE OF THREE KINGS is a book you will want to read again and again. If you would like to know more about the ways and purposes of the cross, suffering and transformation (which must come into the life of all Christians), then you will want to read THE INWARD JOURNEY.

DIVINE LIFE might be looked upon as a technical explanation of the human spirit and its difference from the human soul, but having read this book, you will be pleased to know more about the spiritual process going on inside you. This book is a great help to Christians in their quest to get a handle on their spirit.

THE EARLY CHURCH, Volume I, the story of the body of Christ from Pentecost to Antioch, will give you insight into what "church life" meant in the first century.

THE TORCH OF THE TESTIMONY tells the story of the church and church life as it survived during the dark ages and beyond.

The following prices are for the year 1985 *only*; please write for our catalog for price update and for new releases.

The Divine Romance (Edwards)...................... (10.95 hb) 7.95 pb
Experiencing the Depths of
    Jesus Christ (Guyon)... 4.95
The Spiritual Adventure (Guyon)................................ 7.95
Practicing His Presence (Lawrence)............................ 4.95
The Inward Journey (Edwards).................................. 5.95
A Tale of Three Kings (Edwards)................................ 5.95
The Spiritual Guide (Molinos)................................... 5.95
Guyon's Letters.. 6.95
Fenelon's Letters.. 5.95
The Early Church (Edwards).................................... 4.95
Torch of the Testimony (Kennedy).............................. 6.95
Our Mission (Edwards).. 8.95
Letters to A Devastated Christian (Edwards).................... 3.95
Guyon's Commentaries:
    Genesis 5.95
    Exodus (The Way Out)....................................... 7.95
    Song of Songs.. 5.95
    Job.. 7.95
    Revelation (Christ Our Revelation).......................... 8.95
The Biography of Mme. Guyon (Upham)......................... 8.95

Christian Books

Publishing House

Box 959

Gardiner, Maine 04345

207-582-4880

Visa-Mastercard accepted